ELECTRICITY AND MAGNETISM

FUNDAMENTALS

Other books in the FUNdamental Series
Light FUNdamentals
Heat FUNdamentals
Mechanics FUNdamentals
Sound FUNdamentals

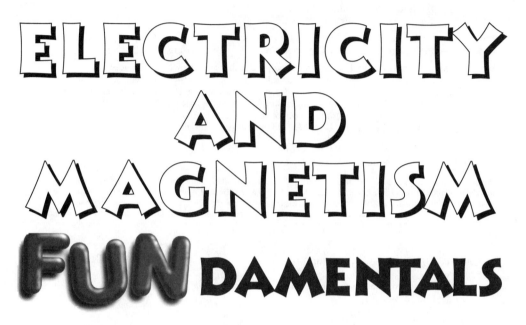

ELECTRICITY AND MAGNETISM FUNDAMENTALS

FUNtastic Science Activities for Kids

Robert W. Wood

Illustrated by Bill Wright

LEARNING TRIANGLE PRESS

*Connecting
kids, parents, and teachers
through learning*

An imprint of McGraw-Hill

New York San Francisco Washington, D.C. Auckland Bogotá Caracas
Lisbon London Madrid Mexico City Milan Montreal New Delhi
San Juan Singapore Sydney Tokyo Toronto

McGraw-Hill

A Division of The **McGraw·Hill** Companies

©1997 by **The McGraw-Hill Companies, Inc.**
Published by Learning Triangle Press, an imprint of McGraw-Hill.

pbk   1 2 3 4 5 6 7 8 9 FGR/FGR 9 0 0 9 8 7 6
hc   1 2 3 4 5 6 7 8 9 FGR/FGR 9 0 0 9 8 7 6

Product or brand names used in this book may be trade names or trademarks. Where we believe that there may be proprietary claims to such trade names or trademarks, the name has been used with an initial capital or it has been capitalized in the style used by the name claimant. Regardless of the capitalization used, all such names have been used in an editorial manner without any intent to convey endorsement of or other affiliation with the name claimant. Neither the author nor the publisher intends to express any judgment as to the validity or legal status of any such proprietary claims.

Library of Congress Cataloging-in-Publication Data
Wood, Robert W.
     Electricity and magnetism FUNdamentals / Robert W. Wood;
illustrated by Bill Wright.
          p. cm. — (FUNtastic science activities for kids)
     Summary: Provides instructions for a variety of experiments to
demonstrate the nature of electricity and magnetism and the
relationship between them.
     ISBN 0-07-071804-0 (hc). — ISBN 0-07-071805-9 (sc)
     1. Electricity—Experiments—Juvenile literature. 2. Magnetism—
Experiments—Juvenile literature. [1. Electricity—Experiments.
2. Magnetism—Experiments.   3. Experiments.] I. Wright, Bill, ill.
II. Title.   III. Series: Wood, Robert W.,
FUNtastic science activities for kids.
QC527.2.W657 1996
537'.078—dc20   96-41797
                                                                          CIP
                                                                          AC

McGraw-Hill books are available at special quantity discounts to use as premiums and sales promotions, or for use in corporate training programs. For more information, please write to the Director of Special Sales, McGraw-Hill, 11 West 19th Street, New York, NY 10011. Or contact your local bookstore.

Acquisitions editor: Kim Tabor
Editorial team: Managing Editor: Susan Kagey
                  Book editor: Joanne M. Slike
                  Technical reviewer: Andrea T. Bennett
Production team: DTP Supervisor: Pat Caruso
                  DTP Operators: Tanya Howden, Kim Sheran, John Lovell
                  DTP Computer Artist Supervisor: Tess Raynor
                  DTP Computer Artists: Nora Ananos, Charles Burkhour, Steven Jay Gellert,
                     Charles Nappa
                  Indexer: Jodi L. Tyler
Designer: Jaclyn J. Boone

CONTENTS

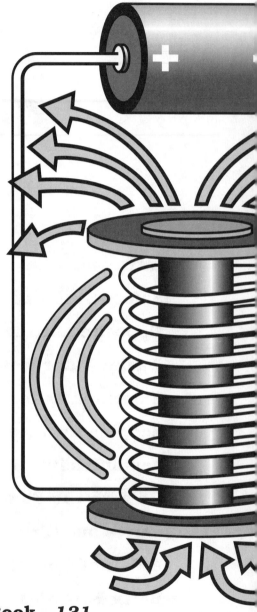

INTRO

This book opens the door to one of the most exciting fields in science—the study of electricity and magnetism. Experiments in electricity can be traced back to 600, when the Greek Thales of Miletus rubbed amber (a brown or yellow translucent, or see-through fossil resin) and silk together to produce static electricity. In fact, the word *electricity* comes from the Greek word *elektron*, which means "amber."

Static electricity is a charge that builds up on something and is waiting for some suitable connection to discharge—like between the clouds and earth during a thunderstorm. *Current electricity* is an electrical current moving along a wire. When any electrical current flows, it develops an invisible force around it called a *magnetic field*.

To understand electricity, you need to know something about the relationship of electricity and magnetism. The two subjects are closely related. Electricity can produce magnetism, and magnetism can produce electricity. Understanding their relationship has led to the development of most of today's entertaining and labor-saving devices. Our imaginations are the only limit to exciting discoveries in the future.

The experiments in this book are a basic introduction to the study of electricity and magnetism. You'll learn what electricity and magnetism are, where they come from, and some of the ways you can use them. Each experiment begins with an objective, followed by a materials list and step-by-step procedures. Results are given to explain what is being demonstrated, as well as a few questions for further discussion. Each experiment concludes with fun facts to educate and entertain.

Where measurements are used, they are given in both the English and metric systems as numbers that will make the experiments easy to perform. Use whichever system you like, but realize that the numbers might not be exact equivalents.

Be sure to read Safety Stuff before you begin any experiment. It recommends safety precautions you should take. It also tells you whether you should have a teacher or another adult help you. Keep safety in mind, and you will have a rewarding first experience in the exciting world of physics.

SAFETY
STUFF

Science experiments can be fun and exciting, but safety should always be considered. Parents and teachers are encouraged to participate with their children and students.

 Look over the steps before beginning any experiment. You will notice that some steps are preceded by a caution symbol like the one next to this paragraph. This symbol means that you should use extra safety precautions or that the experiment requires adult supervision.

Materials or tools used in some experiments could be dangerous in young hands. Adult supervision is recommended whenever the caution symbol appears. Children need to be taught about the care and handling of sharp tools or combustible or toxic materials and how to protect surfaces. Also, extreme caution must be exercised around any open flame or very hot surface.

Use common sense and make safety the priority, and you will have a safe and fun experience!

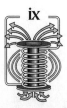

X

Definitely a sticky situation!

OPPOSITES ATTRACT

YOUR CHALLENGE

To investigate the conditions that create static electricity and observe its effect on small objects.

Note: Experiments with static electricity work best when the air is dry. Try this experiment on a dry day, then a humid day, and compare the results.

DO THIS

1   Wash the comb with warm, soapy water to remove any oil, then shake off any drops of water.

2   Tie one end of the thread to the piece of puffed rice. (Figure 1-1)

3   Tie the other end of the thread to a support so that the cereal is free to swing like a pendulum. (Figure 1-2)

YOU NEED

Hard rubber or nylon comb

Piece of puffed rice cereal

Piece of wool cloth

Wide roll of transparent tape

Length of sewing thread about 2 feet (60 cm) long

1

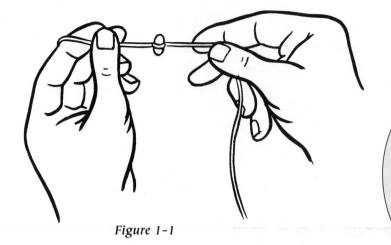

Figure 1-1

Tie the cereal to one end of the thread.

Steady, now. This isn't as easy as it looks!

Suspend the cereal so that it is free to swing.

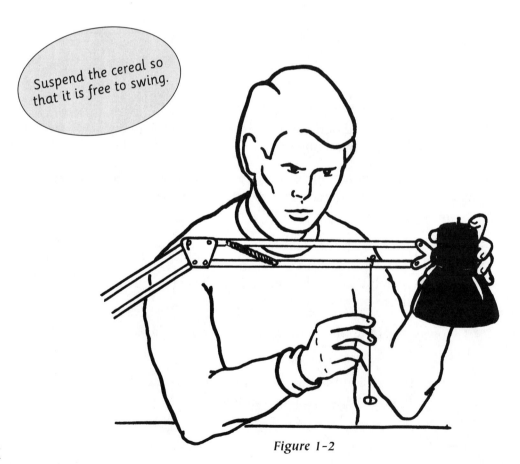

Figure 1-2

2

4   Rub the comb briskly with the wool cloth, and slowly bring one end of the comb near the suspended cereal. If the comb and wool cloth don't work, quickly pull a short length of transparent tape from its roll, and hold the non-sticky side near the cereal. What happens? (Figure 1-3)

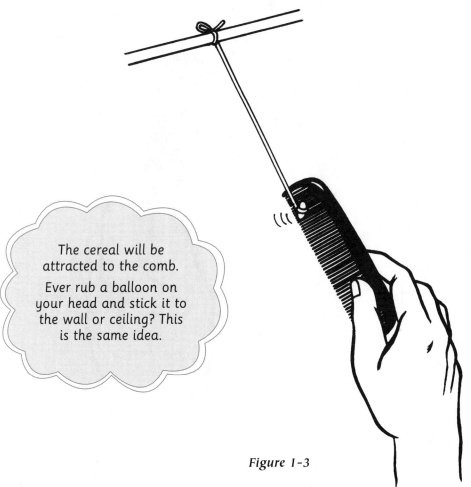

The cereal will be attracted to the comb.

Ever rub a balloon on your head and stick it to the wall or ceiling? This is the same idea.

Figure 1-3

5   Allow the cereal to stay attached to the comb. What happens then? Slowly bring the comb near the cereal again. What does the cereal do now? (Figure 1-4)

6   Next, touch the cereal with the tip of your finger, and bring the comb near the cereal. What happens?

Figure 1-4

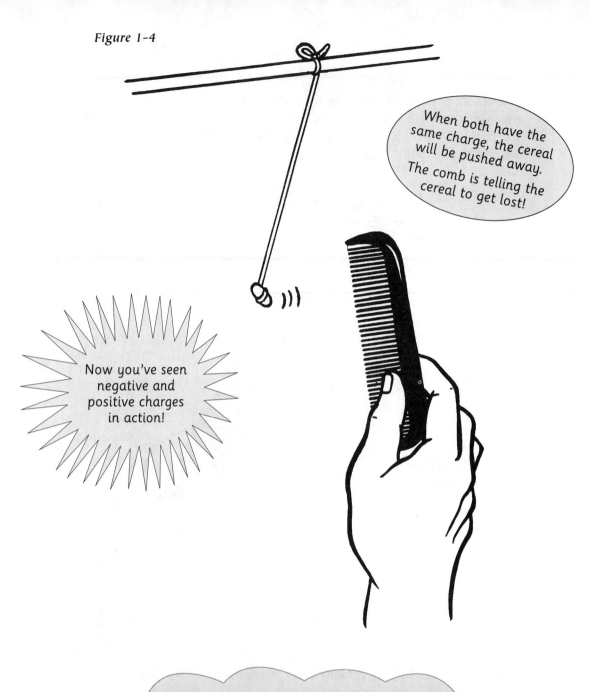

When both have the same charge, the cereal will be pushed away. The comb is telling the cereal to get lost!

Now you've seen negative and positive charges in action!

Here's something fun to do on a cold winter night: When you're lying in bed, try rubbing your knees against the covers, then quickly separate the blanket from the sheet.

What Happened?

Static electricity is electricity at rest, or a buildup of an electrical charge. Did the comb have an electrical charge? Why?

Objects may carry two kinds of charge: positive and negative. Most objects are made of equal amounts of each. If an object contains more negative charges than positive charges, it will have a net negative charge. Rubbing action can pull negative charges from one object to another. When the comb was rubbed by the wool cloth, the negative charge from the wool was transferred to the comb. The negative charges piled up on the comb, giving it an overall negative charge. The wool was left with an overall positive charge.

A charged object attracts an uncharged object or an object with equal negative and positive charges. When an object has equal negative and positive charges, it is *neutral*. The piece of cereal was neutral, so it was attracted to the comb. However, while the cereal was touching the comb, some of the extra negative charges moved from the comb to the cereal. Soon the cereal also built up a net negative charge.

Because both the comb and the cereal are now negatively charged, they push each other away. When you touched the cereal, the surplus negative charges moved from the cereal to your finger. The cereal loses its net negative charge and is again attracted to the comb.

Use the charged comb to pick up bits of paper. What else is attracted to the comb? Must the comb be near the object to attract it? Do you think that the force of the charge decreases when the distance is increased? Do fabrics from a clothes dryer have an electrical charge?

The electrical charges in this experiment are very small. Can you think of more powerful electrical charges? Do you think static electricity could be dangerous? Could a spark from static electricity start a fire? Is lightning a form of static electricity?

GUESS WHAT ?

⭐ *If conditions are just right, scuffing your shoes on a carpet can build up a charge of up to 20,000 volts. The charge can produce a painful but harmless shock because of the low current.*

⭐ *The spark plug in powered lawn mowers produces a spark of more than 10,000 volts.*

Guaranteed to give you a charge!

WACKY WATER WONDERS

YOUR CHALLENGE

To observe how a small electrical charge affects running water.

DO THIS

1 Turn on the cold water faucet and adjust the flow to a narrow stream of water.

2 Rub the comb briskly with a wool cloth or run it through your hair several times. (Figure 2-1)

3 Now hold the comb near the stream of water. If the comb doesn't work, try pulling a short length of transparent tape from the roll. (Figure 2-2)

4 Hold the tape near the stream of water. What do you see?

YOU NEED

Dry day with low humidity

Clean, dry plastic or nylon comb, or a clear, wide roll of transparent tape

Running water

7

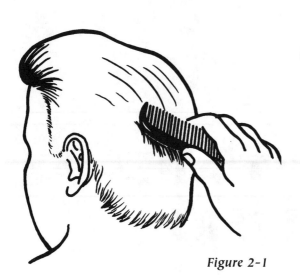

Rub the comb briskly.
Try rubbing it on
your head for a
hair-raising experience!

Figure 2-1

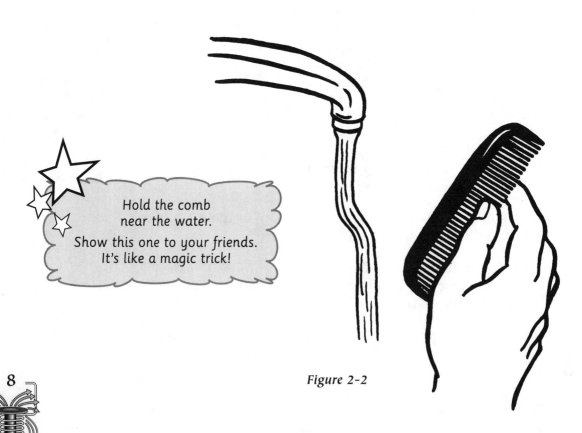

Hold the comb
near the water.
Show this one to your friends.
It's like a magic trick!

Figure 2-2

8

What Happened?

When you rubbed the comb, it built up an electrical charge. The water was either not charged or it was neutral. Electrically charged objects attract objects that have an opposite or neutral charge.

Do you think that being able to direct a stream of water by static electricity could be useful? Could static electricity be used to control other fluids such as paint? If a car body was charged with static electricity, could an even coating of protective material be applied?

Guess What?

★ *Benjamin Franklin was the first to suggest that static electricity has a positive and negative charge.*

★ *In industrial areas, electrically charged plates inside a smokestack can trap polluting particles.*

Here's another wild
and woolly one!

ELECTRONS AGLOW!

YOUR CHALLENGE

To produce light without a filament. *Fluorescent* lights do
not have wires, called *filaments*, inside them like regular
incandescent bulbs. With a regular bulb, electricity heats the
filament to the point that it glows and produces light.

DO THIS

 1   Make sure the lamp is turned off and unplugged. Then
carefully remove the tube from a fluorescent lamp or
ask an adult for help. Take it into a darkened room.
(Figure 3-1)

2   Vigorously rub the tube with the wool cloth. What
happens? (Figure 3-2)

YOU NEED

Darkened room

**Fluorescent tube from
a fluorescent lamp**

Piece of wool cloth

11

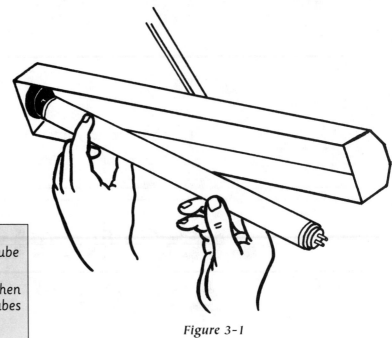

Remove the fluorescent tube from the lamp.

Be sure to ask for help when doing this. Fluorescent tubes can be dangerous.

Figure 3-1

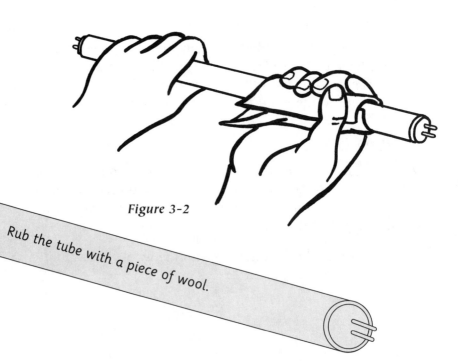

Figure 3-2

Rub the tube with a piece of wool.

What Happened?

The friction between the wool and the glass tube caused negative charges to strike and dislodge similar charges from a gas inside the tube. These dislodged charges give off ultraviolet rays. These rays strike the special coating, called *phosphor*, on the inside of the glass tube, which causes the coating to glow and give off light.

About 90 percent of electrical energy used to make an incandescent lightbulb light ends up as heat. Do you think this is an efficient use of energy, or should these bulbs be used as heaters instead? Fluorescent lamps produce more light for less energy than incandescent bulbs. Do you think that fluorescent lamps burn much cooler?

If the phosphor coatings inside a fluorescent tube are changed, other types of light will be produced. One such type imitates sunlight and can be used to grow plants. Can you think of some practical uses for this type of fluorescent light?

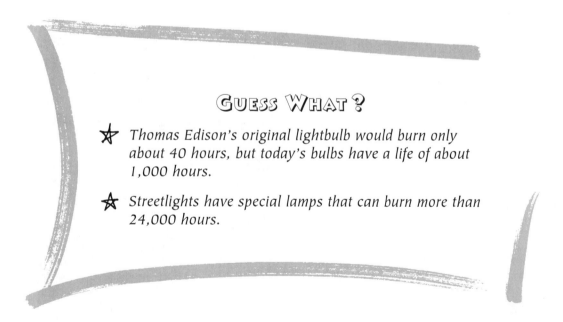

Guess What?

★ *Thomas Edison's original lightbulb would burn only about 40 hours, but today's bulbs have a life of about 1,000 hours.*

★ *Streetlights have special lamps that can burn more than 24,000 hours.*

SCOPING FOR ELECTRONS

YOUR CHALLENGE

To create a device, called an *electroscope,* to detect static electricity.

DO THIS

1 Straighten one end of the paper clip and bend it at a right angle to support the strip of aluminum foil. The other end of the paper clip should be able to be clamped onto the side of the glass. (Figure 4-1)

> Bend the paper clip so that it will clamp on the rim of the glass.

YOU NEED

Metal paper clip

Narrow strip of aluminum foil about ⅛ x 2 inches (3mm x 5 cm)

Clear drinking glass

Clean, dry plastic or nylon comb, or a roll of wide transparent tape

Piece of wool

Figure 4-1

15

2   Bend the aluminum foil in half and drape it over the end of the paper clip. The halves of the aluminum foil should be in line and can even be touching each other, but not the bottom or sides of the glass. (Figure 4-2)

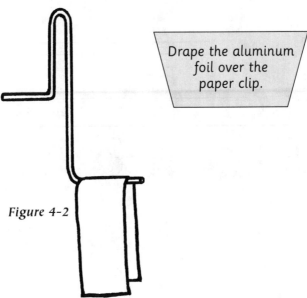

Drape the aluminum foil over the paper clip.

Figure 4-2

3   Slide the other end of the paper clip onto the rim of the glass. (Figure 4-3)

Mount the paper clip on the glass.

Remember, the foil shouldn't touch the glass.

Figure 4-3

4 Now rub the comb vigorously with the wool and touch the comb to the paper clip. What did you see? (*Note:* Another way to build up a charge is to quickly unroll a short length of transparent tape, then touch the non-sticky side of the tape to the paper clip.) (Figure 4-4)

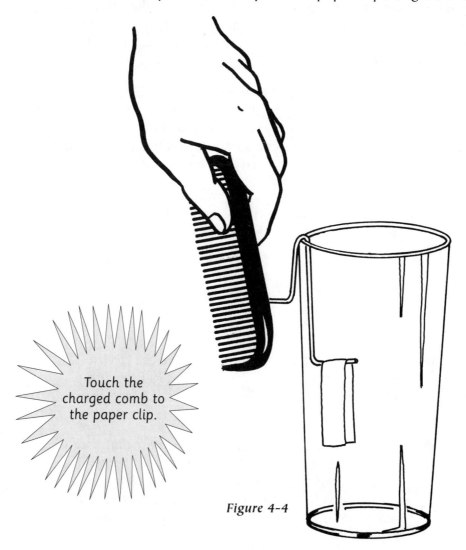

Touch the charged comb to the paper clip.

Figure 4-4

What Happened?

Electrons, which are negative charges, moved from the comb, down the paper clip, and charged the aluminum strips. The strips have an excess

17

of electrons, so they both have a negative charge and repel each other. Take the comb away, and the strips will gradually fall back again as the surplus of electrons travel back up the wire and leak into the air.

A glass rod rubbed with a piece of silk will produce the same effect, except the strips will have a positive charge. The glass attracted electrons from the strips, leaving them with an excess of positive charges, or *protons*.

Try testing other objects for static charges. Begin by charging the electroscope with wool and the comb. This charges it negatively. When you bring a charged object near the paper clip and the strips continue to spread apart, you know the object also has a negative charge. But if the object causes the strips to move together, the object has a positive charge.

Until lately, proton and electron charges were thought to be the smallest charges, but scientists now believe that smaller charges occur and that they are properties of the subatomic particles called *quarks*.

GUESS WHAT ?

⭐ *Electrostatic charges are used to guide the electron beam in a television tube. The beam produces the picture by repeatedly sweeping across the face of the tube in only a fraction of a second.*

⭐ *Robert Van de Graaff invented a generator that used a motor-driven silk belt to produce static electricity. The Van de Graaff generator could develop a charge of millions of volts. It was used for research during the 1930s and is now on display in the Smithsonian Institution.*

No sourpusses allowed!

LEMONTRICITY?

YOUR CHALLENGE

To make a simple wet cell battery.

DO THIS

1   Roll and press the lemon on a table to make it juicy. Then place the lemon on the paper towel to absorb the excess juice. (Figure 5-1)

YOU NEED

Lemon

Paper towel

Small nail

Knife

Copper penny

DC voltmeter

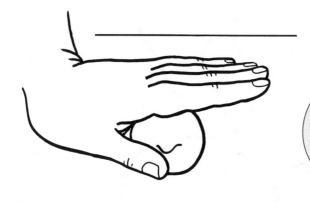

Roll the lemon back and forth on the counter.

The lemon should be nice and squishy.

Figure 5-1

2 Carefully press the nail into the side of the lemon. (Figure 5-2)

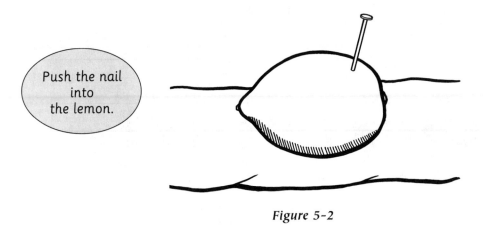

Push the nail into the lemon.

Figure 5-2

⚠ 3 Carefully cut a small slit about an inch (2.54 cm) from the nail and insert the penny. (Never cut with an object held against yourself. You could slip and seriously injure yourself.) (Figure 5-3)

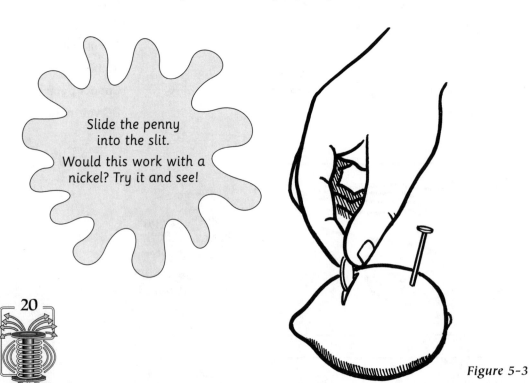

Slide the penny into the slit.

Would this work with a nickel? Try it and see!

Figure 5-3

4 Touch the positive lead from the voltmeter to the penny and the negative lead to the nail. (Figure 5-4)

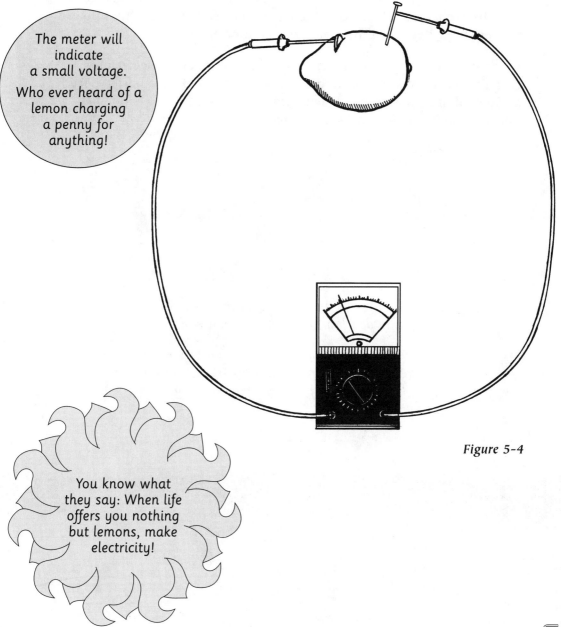

The meter will indicate a small voltage.

Who ever heard of a lemon charging a penny for anything!

You know what they say: When life offers you nothing but lemons, make electricity!

Figure 5-4

5 Check the reading on the voltmeter.

What Happened?

The citric acid in the lemon acted as the solution in a wet cell battery. The copper wire became positively charged, and the steel wire became negatively charged. The acid in the lemon released electrons that flowed through the wires when the meter was connected.

What other foods contain an acid that could conduct an electrical current? Try using a potato, a tomato, or grapes to make a battery. Try a spoonful of table salt moistened with warm water. What happens? Compare the amount of volts from each one.

How many things in your home use batteries?

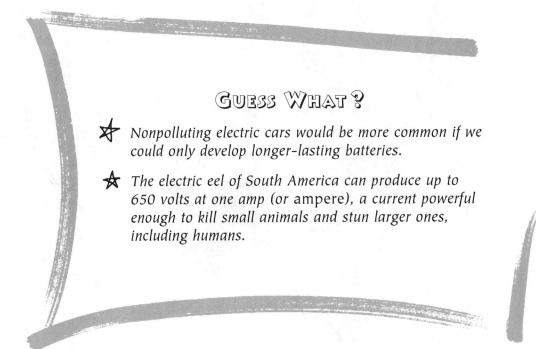

Guess What?

★ *Nonpolluting electric cars would be more common if we could only develop longer-lasting batteries.*

★ *The electric eel of South America can produce up to 650 volts at one amp (or ampere), a current powerful enough to kill small animals and stun larger ones, including humans.*

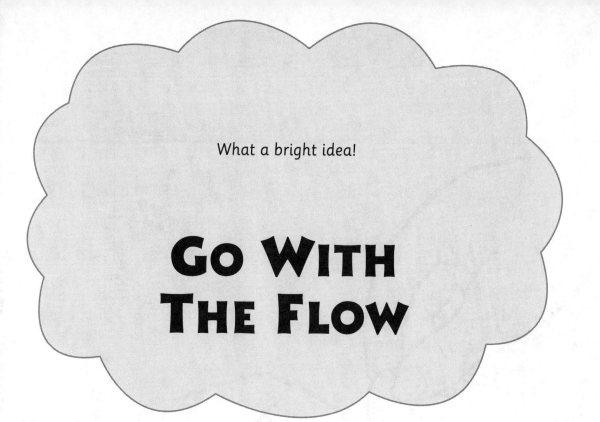

What a bright idea!

Go With The Flow

Your Challenge

To make electricity flow.

 Note: A cord from an old lamp can provide copper wire for experiments. The wires inside are stranded and easy to work with. Have an adult carefully strip the insulation away for you.

Do This

1   Twist one end of the copper wire tightly around the metal part of the lightbulb. Stand the battery upright on a table, with the bottom of the battery resting on the other end of the copper wire. (Figure 6-1)

2   Touch the metal point of the bottom of the bulb to the top of the battery. What happens? (Figure 6-2)

3   Remove the bulb. Now what do you see?

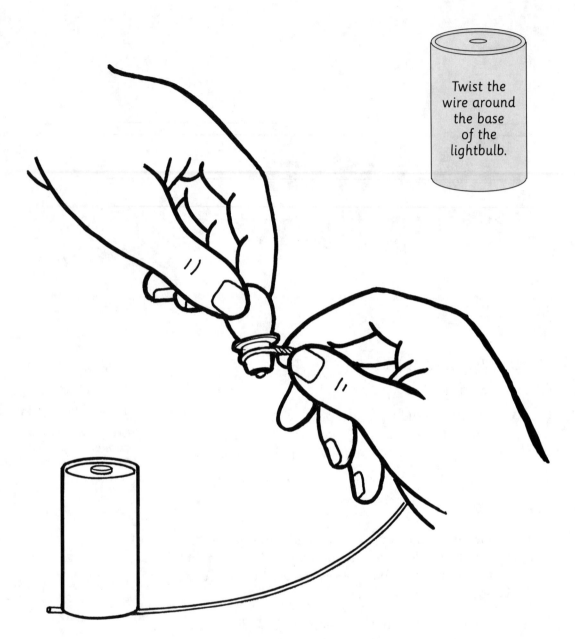

Twist the wire around the base of the lightbulb.

Figure 6-1

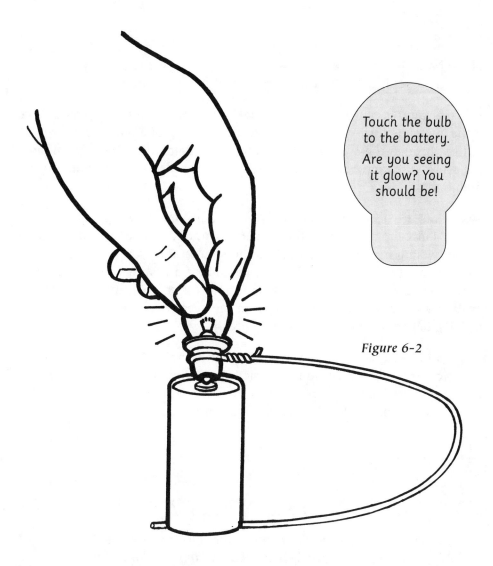

Touch the bulb to the battery.

Are you seeing it glow? You should be!

Figure 6-2

WHAT HAPPENED ?

The top of the battery and the center point on the bottom of the bulb take the place of the switch in an electrical circuit. When you touched the bulb to the battery, you closed the switch. The lightbulb is considered the *circuit load*, and the battery is the *power source*. In order for electricity to flow (forming an electric current), there must be a closed path.

When the light burned, current flowed out the bottom of the battery, through the wire, and to the side of the bulb. Then it traveled through the

25

filament inside the bulb, out the bottom of the bulb, and back into the top of the battery. This makes a closed path or electric circuit. Any break along the circuit will stop the current, and the light will not burn.

When a lamp is plugged into an outlet, it is connected to a power source. If the switch is turned on, the current flows along one wire from the outlet, through the switch, then through the filament in the bulb, along the other wire, and back to the outlet. This completes the circuit, and the bulb lights.

Two wires are necessary to complete a circuit: one wire coming from the power source to a load (lightbulb, electric motor, and so on), and another wire traveling from the load back to the source. Can you imagine the two wires coming from the electric company, miles away, to your home? A third wire, called a *ground wire,* is important for safety. It provides an easier path for the electrical current in the event of a short circuit. (Refer to the glossary for more on ground wires.)

How would you buy groceries or heat your home without electricity? Could a car be driven without electricity? Imagine life in the previous century before electrical appliances. How did people heat water for cooking or bathing? How did people read at night?

GUESS WHAT ?

★ *Electric companies cannot store electricity. When you turn on an appliance such as a lamp or clothes dryer, the power plant instantly sees this increase in electrical consumption and must respond with a larger supply.*

★ *Emergency facilities such as airports and hospitals have backup systems in case of a power failure. These systems sense a power failure and automatically switch on the emergency power of batteries or generators.*

We go full circuit in this experiment.

SERIES-OUS CIRCUITRY!

YOUR CHALLENGE

To connect lights in a series circuit.

DO THIS

 1 Have an adult remove about 2 inches (5 cm) of insulation from the ends of each wire with the knife or clippers.

2 Use the screwdriver to loosen the terminal screws on the bulb holders. Loop the bare ends of one wire around one of the screws on each bulb holder and tighten the screws. (Figure 7-1)

3 Connect one end of the remaining two wires to the other screws on the bulb holders and tighten the screws. You now should have the holders connected in a line with two wires to use for leads to the battery. (Figure 7-2)

YOU NEED

Knife or nail clippers

Flashlight battery

Two threaded-base flashlight bulbs

Two threaded-base bulb holders

Small screwdriver

Three small insulated copper wires about 7 inches (18 cm) long

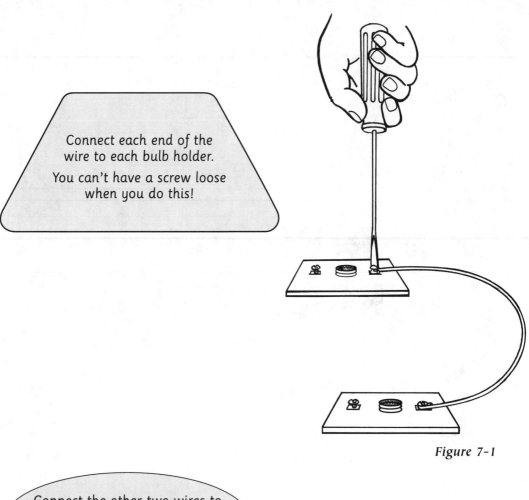

Connect each end of the wire to each bulb holder.

You can't have a screw loose when you do this!

Figure 7-1

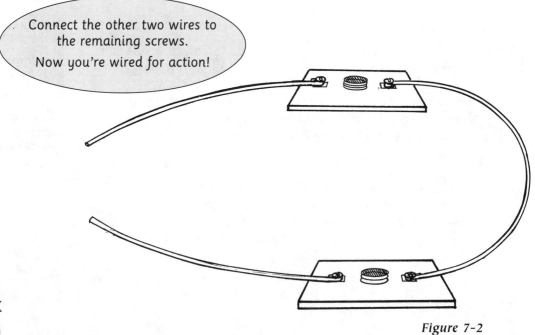

Connect the other two wires to the remaining screws.

Now you're wired for action!

28

Figure 7-2

4 Screw the bulbs into each holder. Touch the wire leads to opposite ends of the battery. What happens? (Figure 7-3)

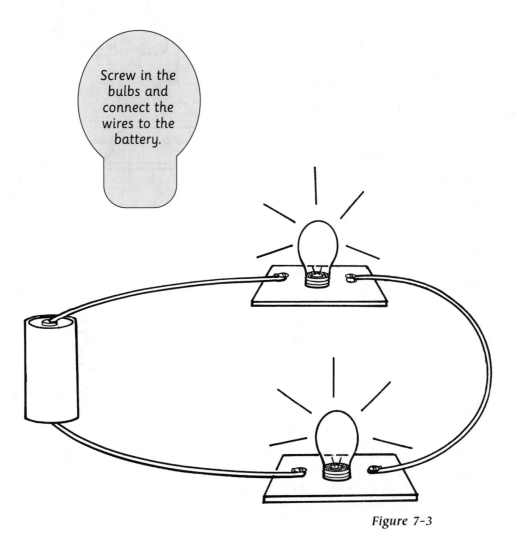

Screw in the bulbs and connect the wires to the battery.

Figure 7-3

5 Disconnect the battery and remove one of the bulbs. Reconnect the battery. Now what do you see? (Figure 7-4)

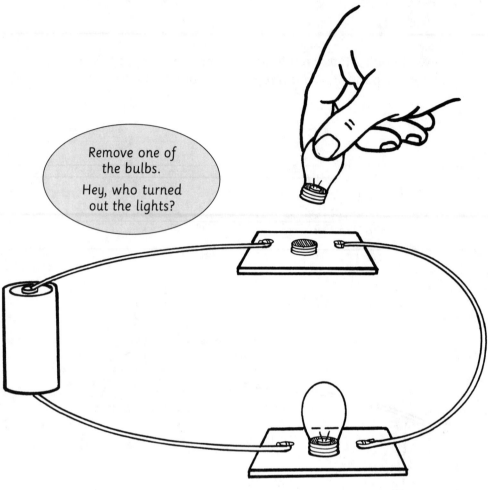

Remove one of the bulbs.

Hey, who turned out the lights?

Figure 7-4

WHAT HAPPENED?

Electrons flowed from the bottom of the battery, through the lead wire to the holder, and through the filament of the first bulb. Then the current flowed through the connecting wire to the other bulb, and on back to the top of the battery. The circuit was complete, which allowed the bulbs to burn.

When the battery was disconnected, the circuit opened. The electrons couldn't flow, and the bulbs could not light. When you removed one of the bulbs, the circuit opened, and the remaining bulb could not light. This is one of the characteristics of a *series circuit*. If a bulb burns out or if a break occurs in a wire, all of the lights go out.

30

In a series circuit, the current is exactly the same throughout the circuit, but the source voltage is divided between each bulb. Therefore, the more bulbs you have, the lower the brightness of each bulb.

Wiring devices in series is practical if low amounts of voltage are needed and when the current through each device must be the same. Can you think of any advantage for wiring lights in a series circuit?

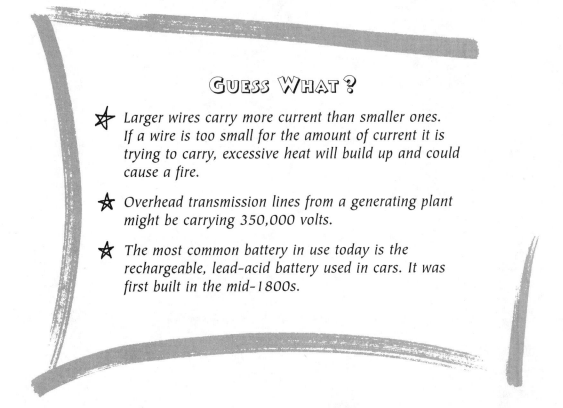

GUESS WHAT?

⭐ *Larger wires carry more current than smaller ones. If a wire is too small for the amount of current it is trying to carry, excessive heat will build up and could cause a fire.*

⭐ *Overhead transmission lines from a generating plant might be carrying 350,000 volts.*

⭐ *The most common battery in use today is the rechargeable, lead-acid battery used in cars. It was first built in the mid-1800s.*

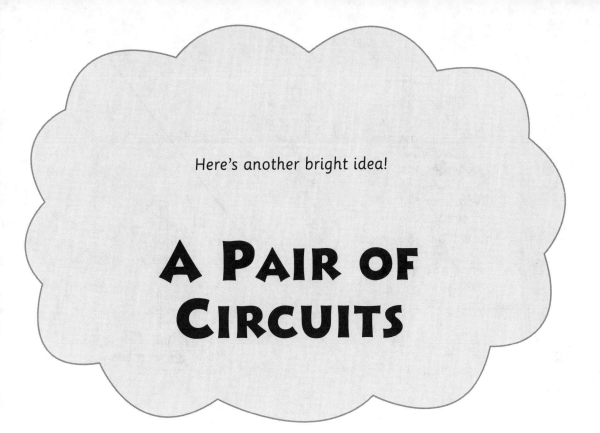

Here's another bright idea!

A PAIR OF CIRCUITS

YOUR CHALLENGE

To connect lights in a parallel circuit and to compare this circuit with lights wired in a series circuit

DO THIS

 1   Have an adult remove about 2 inches (5 cm) of insulation from the ends of each wire with the knife or nail clippers.

2   Use the screwdriver to loosen the terminal screws on the bulb holders. Twist the bare ends of two wires together and connect them to one of the bulb holders. (Figure 8-1)

3   Twist the ends of the remaining two wires together and connect them to the other screw of the same holder. You now should have two wires connected to one holder and four wires with free ends. (Figure 8-2)

4   Connect two free ends to the screws to the other holder and screw in the bulbs. Touch the remaining leads to the battery. What happens? (Figure 8-3)

YOU NEED

Knife or nail clippers

Four small insulated copper wires about 7 inches (18 cm) long

Flashlight battery

Two threaded-base flashlight bulbs

Two threaded-base bulb holders

Small screwdriver

33

Twist two wires together and connect them to one of the screws.

This will get you twisting and turning!

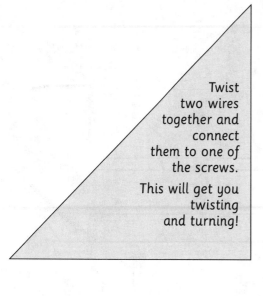

Figure 8-1

Twist the other two wires together and connect them to the remaining screw.

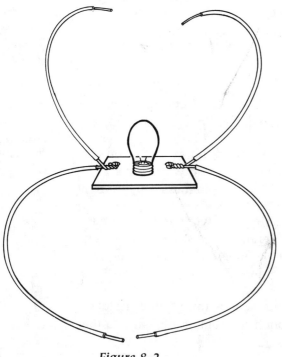

Figure 8-2

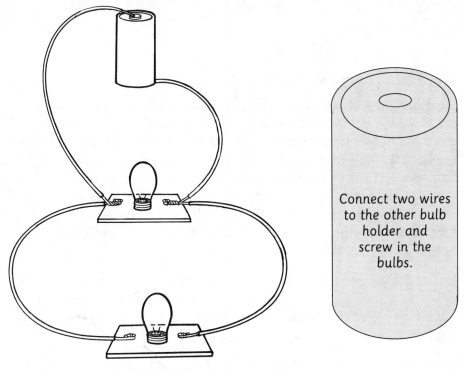

Connect two wires to the other bulb holder and screw in the bulbs.

Figure 8-3

5   Disconnect the battery and remove one of the bulbs. Reconnect the battery. Now what do you see? (Figure 8-4)

Remove one of the bulbs. Is the bulb still lit?

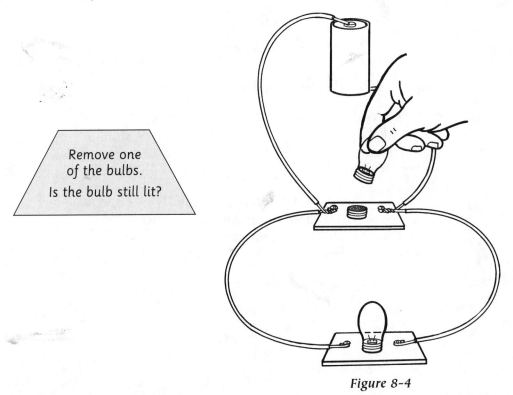

Figure 8-4

WHAT HAPPENED?

Electrons flowed from the bottom of the battery, through the lead wire to the first bulb holder, and through the filament of the first bulb. Because the other holder is connected to the same terminals as the wires going to the battery, the second bulb received the same voltage as the first. When you removed one of the bulbs, the remaining bulb continued to receive the full voltage and kept burning. The bulbs wired in this manner represent two branch, or parallel, circuits. In a *parallel circuit*, each branch receives the same amount of voltage, but the current is divided between each branch.

In a series circuit, the *current* is the same at every point in the circuit. In parallel circuits, the *voltage* is the same at every point in the circuit. Our homes are wired in parallel circuits in order for all of the lights or appliances to receive the same amount of voltage.

If one light burns out in a car, do all of the lights go out? Do you think cars are wired in parallel or series circuits? Could the metal frame of a car be used as a return path for the electrical current? Would you expect schools and factories to use parallel or series wiring? Why?

GUESS WHAT?

★ *Unlike series circuits, the more appliances plugged into a parallel circuit, the greater the current. This stronger current can cause an overload and blow a fuse or "trip" a circuit breaker.*

★ Ground-fault circuit interrupters (GFCIs) are special safety outlets found in bathrooms and kitchens. Their breakers will "trip" in about one-fortieth of a second to prevent dangerous shock.

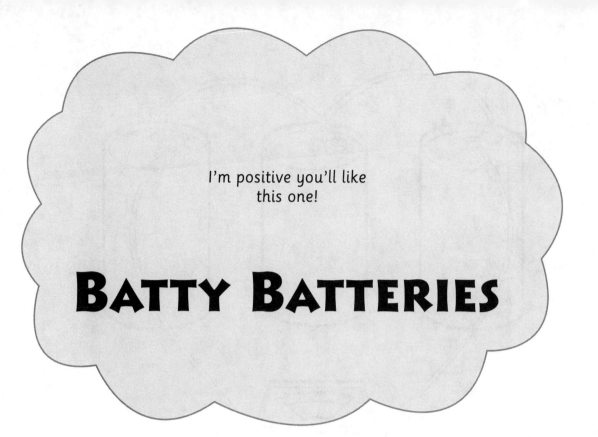

I'm positive you'll like
this one!

BATTY BATTERIES

YOUR CHALLENGE

To compare the voltage produced by batteries in a series circuit and batteries in a parallel circuit.

DO THIS

1 Stand the batteries upright in a row. Connect a wire from the negative terminal of the first battery to the positive terminal of the second battery.

2 Connect a wire from the negative terminal of the second battery to the positive terminal of the third battery.

3 Connect the positive lead of the voltmeter to the positive terminal of the first battery. Connect the negative lead of the voltmeter to the negative terminal of the third battery. What is the meter reading? (Figure 9-1)

YOU NEED

Three batteries with screw terminals, such as lantern batteries

Three copper wires about 7 inches (18 cm) long

DC voltmeter

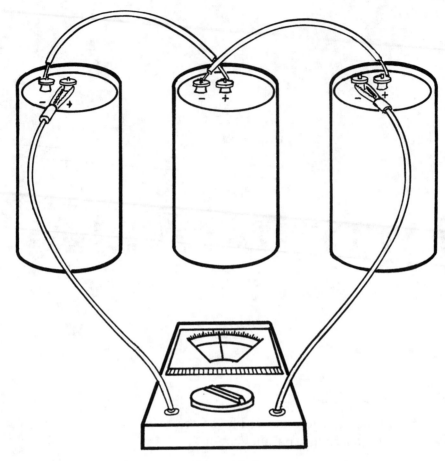

Figure 9-1

Connect the two wires between the negative and positive
terminals of each battery.

Did you know that the voltmeter is named for
Conte Alessandro Giuseppe Antonio Anastasio Volta, an Italian physicist?
You can call him Mr. Volta, for short!

4   Disconnect all wires.

5   Now connect a wire from the positive terminal of the first battery to
    the positive terminal of the second battery. Then connect a wire
    from the positive terminal of the second battery to the positive
    terminal of the third battery.

6   Connect a wire from the negative terminal of the first battery to the negative terminal of the second battery. Then connect a wire from the negative terminal of the second battery to the negative terminal of the third battery. (Figure 9-2)

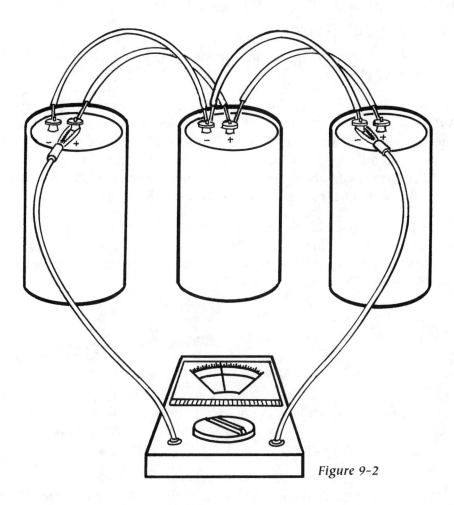

Figure 9-2

Connect the three negative terminals together, then connect the three positive terminals together.

Pay close attention. This part's a little confusing.

7 Connect the meter to the negative and positive terminals of one of the batteries. Connect the positive lead of the voltmeter to the positive terminal of one of the batteries. Then connect the negative lead of the voltmeter to the negative terminal of one of the batteries. What is the meter reading?

WHAT HAPPENED?

Compare the two readings. Which connections provided the higher reading? Why?

If a flashlight uses more than one battery, are they connected in series? What would happen if one of the batteries was accidentally reversed? Is it important to match the size (voltage) of the bulb with the total number of batteries in a flashlight? What would you expect would happen if too small, or too large, a bulb was used? If you connected 12 car batteries (12 volts each) in series, could you light a common lightbulb?

Some factories use electric forklifts with parallel circuits to move materials. Can you think of any other uses for batteries connected in parallel? Would an electric car need batteries connected in parallel? Could common headlamps be used?

GUESS WHAT?

★ Flashlights were being used in about 1900, and at that time the United States was producing about 2 million batteries a year.

★ Large trucks and some diesel cars use batteries connected in parallel because they need a lot of current for starting.

Time for a break in the action!

SHORT CIRCUIT

YOUR CHALLENGE

To construct a short circuit and observe what happens.

DO THIS

1   Loosen the two screw terminals on the bulb holder. Connect the bare ends of two copper wires to each of the terminals and tighten the screws. (Figure 10-1)

2   On the bottom of the bulb holder you will find the ends of the two screw terminals. Twist the bare ends of one of the wires around the ends of these screws, making a connection between the two screws. You now should have a wire lead connected to each terminal and one wire connected between the terminals. (Figure 10-2)

3   Screw in the bulb and briefly touch the ends of the lead wires to the top and bottom of the battery. Notice the brightness of the bulb. (Figure 10-3)

Threaded-base bulb holder

Three copper wires

D-cell battery

Threaded-base flashlight bulb

Small screwdriver

41

Connect a wire to each screw.

You should be getting the hang of this by now!

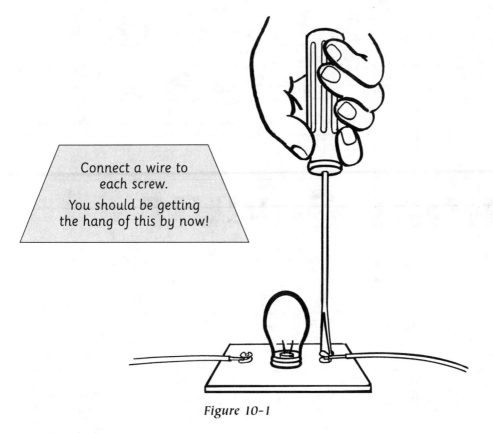

Figure 10-1

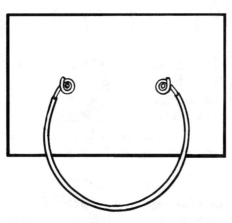

Figure 10-2

Connect one wire to the screws on the bottom of the bulb holder.

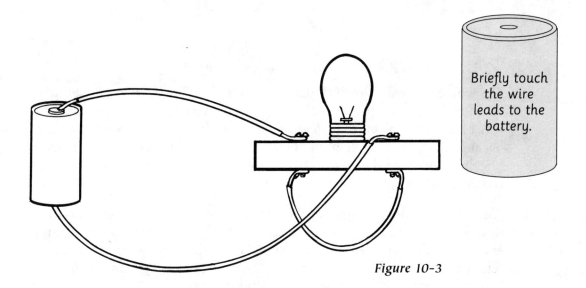

Briefly touch the wire leads to the battery.

Figure 10-3

4   Now disconnect one end of the wire twisted around the screw on the bottom of the holder and reconnect the battery. What do you see? (Figure 10-3)

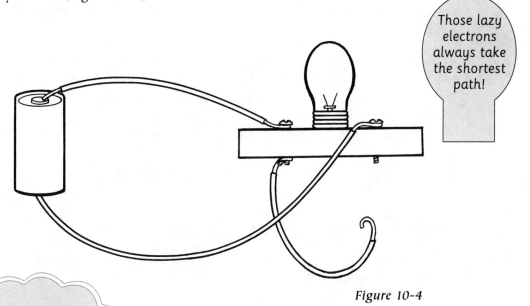

Those lazy electrons always take the shortest path!

Figure 10-4

Disconnect the wire on the bottom. Now let's see WATT happens.

What Happened?

The wire connected directly from one terminal to the other on the bottom of the bulb holder represents a short across the circuit. When the battery was connected, the current ran to the filament of the bulb as normal, but because of the resistance of the filament, the easiest way for the current to complete the path was to run directly through the wire between the terminals.

Short circuit simply means that the current found the easiest, but not the desired, path for completing the circuit. What the circuit now represents is a direct connection from one terminal of the battery to the other terminal. When this condition exists, the current flowing from the battery is at its greatest and can soon destroy the battery.

At higher currents, heat immediately starts to build, wires can melt, and fires can start. In your experiment, the bulb just failed to receive the necessary voltage to light or burned only dimly. After you disconnected the short, the current was forced to travel through the filament, so the bulb burned brightly.

Cords to some appliances, such as electric heaters, can overheat and cause the protective covering on the cord, or *insulation*, to become brittle. If the insulation breaks away, what would happen if the two bare wires touch together? What could happen if someone touched these bare wires? Why would it be dangerous if a household pet chewed an electrical cord?

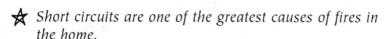

Guess What?

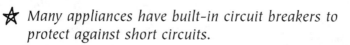

★ Short circuits are one of the greatest causes of fires in the home.

★ Many appliances have built-in circuit breakers to protect against short circuits.

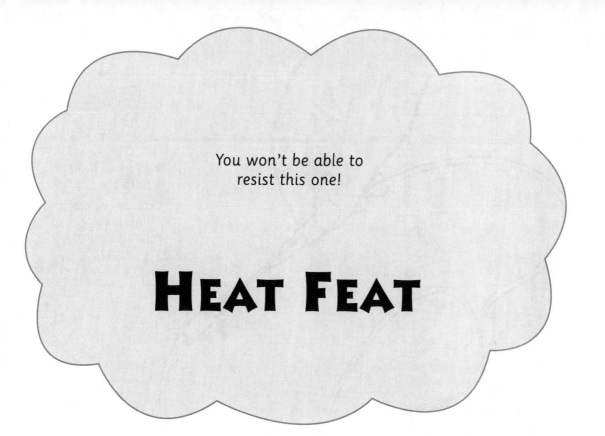

You won't be able to
resist this one!

HEAT FEAT

YOUR CHALLENGE

To generate heat from electricity.

DO THIS

1 Connect a jumper wire to each terminal of the battery.

 2 Connect one insulated clip to one end of the iron wire. *Be sure to keep your fingers on the insulated part. The wire will be hot!*

3 Now touch the free end of the iron wire to the other alligator clip. What happens? (Figure 11-1)

Thin, bare iron wire about 1 inch (2.5 cm) long (such as a strand of picture-frame wire)

6-volt lantern battery

Two jumper wires with insulated alligator clips

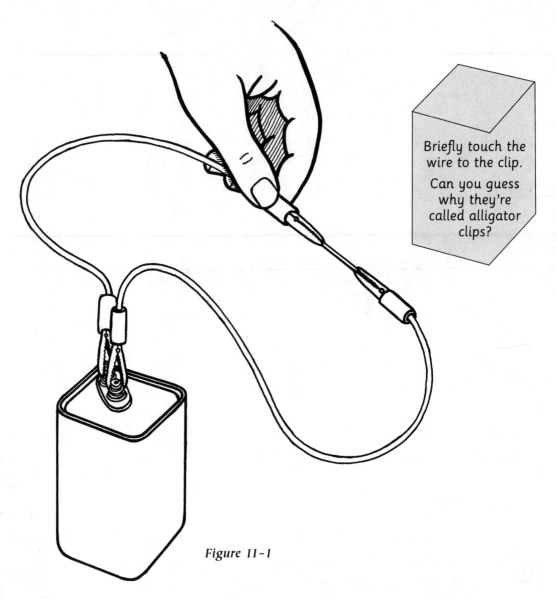

Briefly touch the wire to the clip.

Can you guess why they're called alligator clips?

Figure 11-1

What Happened?

Different types of wire conduct electricity differently. An electrical current flows easily through copper wires, but iron resists the current. This resistance changes the electrical energy into heat.

Heating elements in toasters, electric water heaters, stoves, and other electrical appliances are made of materials that conduct electricity to produce heat. What other uses can you think of for using electricity to produce heat? How do you suppose an electric welder melts metal?

GUESS WHAT?

★ *Heat can also produce electricity. A sensing device called a* thermocouple *in gas water heaters is made up of two different metals. When the pilot light heats these metals, the metals generate a small electrical signal that tells the gas regulator that the pilot light is burning.*

★ *Underground high-voltage transmission cables produce a large amount of heat. They are often installed inside steel pipe containing circulating oil for cooling.*

This experiment can
leave you in the dark.

CONNECTION
PROTECTION

YOUR CHALLENGE

To observe how a fuse can limit the amount of current that
will flow in a circuit.

DO THIS

⚠ 1 Separate the two halves of the lamp
cord. Have an adult carefully trim
about ¼ inch (5mm) of the
insulation from each end with the
knife or clippers. (Figure 12-1)

> Separate the two
> halves of an old
> lamp cord.
>
> It should pull
> apart pretty
> easily.

YOU NEED

**Old lamp cord with
plug about 18 inches
(50 cm) long**

Knife or nail clippers

**Empty cardboard
paper-towel tube**

**Four or five D-cell
batteries**

Aluminum foil

Scissors

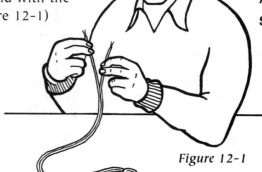

Figure 12-1

49

2 Slide the batteries into the cardboard tube, with all of them pointing in the same direction. This aligns them in a series, with the positive end of one battery touching the negative end of the next battery. The cardboard keeps them from rolling around. (Figure 12-2)

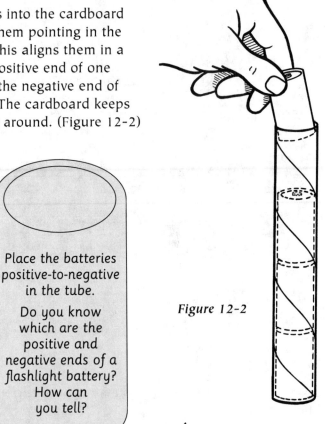

Place the batteries positive-to-negative in the tube.

Do you know which are the positive and negative ends of a flashlight battery? How can you tell?

Figure 12-2

3 With the scissors, cut a very thin sliver of aluminum foil about 4 inches (10 cm) long. Try to cut it as narrow as you can. This will be the fuse. (Figure 12-3)

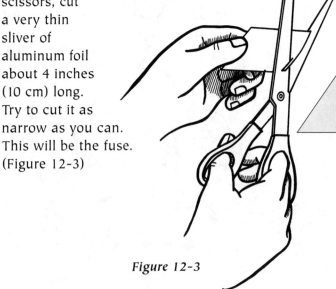

Cut a sliver of aluminum foil.

Remember to cut it as thin as you can.

Figure 12-3

4 Wrap one end of the aluminum foil snugly around one of the prongs of the plug. Then wrap the other end around the other prong. (Figure 12-4)

Connect the strip to the prongs of the plug.

Did you know that aluminum is the most abundant metal in the earth's crust?

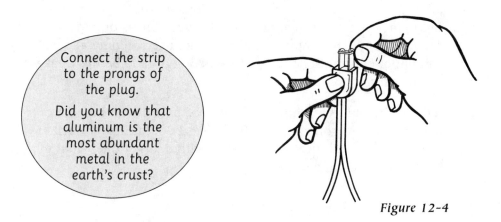

Figure 12-4

5 When the fuse is in place, touch one end of the cord to one end of the batteries, and watch the fuse as you briefly touch the other end of the cord to the other end of the batteries. What do you see? If nothing happens, try a thinner strip of aluminum foil. (Figure 12-5)

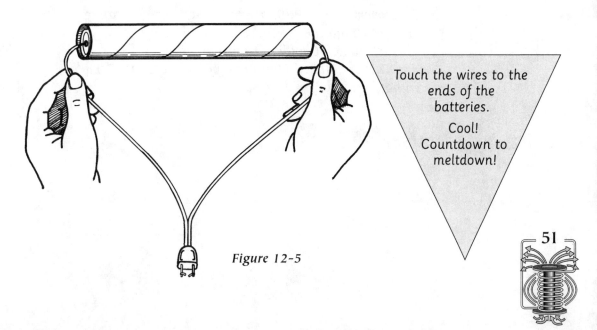

Touch the wires to the ends of the batteries.

Cool! Countdown to meltdown!

Figure 12-5

WHAT HAPPENED?

A normal electrical circuit has a power source, a switch, and a load such as a lightbulb or appliance. The load is a form of *resistance*. The resistance keeps the current from getting too high and starting a fire or causing other damage.

If the load or another spot in the circuit develops a problem that causes the current to increase too much, however, the fuse burns out and stops the flow of electricity. This happens because the fuse will only allow a certain amount of current to flow. The fuse is designed to be the weakest link in the circuit.

Each electrical circuit in your home is protected by a circuit breaker or fuse. Where else would you expect to find fuses? Could they protect circuits in cars? If a small fuse was replaced with a larger one, what might happen? Could this be dangerous?

GUESS WHAT?

★ All of the individual circuits in your home are protected by one main fuse or circuit breaker.

★ On November 9, 1965, a single relay at a generating plant at Niagara Falls caused a major power failure. This left some 30 million people across the northeastern United States and parts of eastern Canada without electricity.

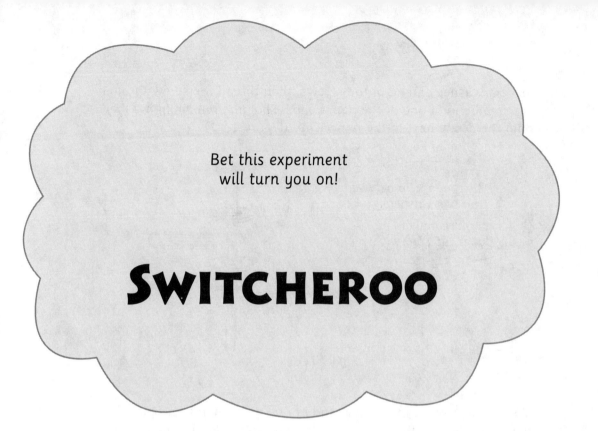

Bet this experiment
will turn you on!

SWITCHEROO

YOUR CHALLENGE

To make a simple switch to use in experiments.

DO THIS

 1 Use the hammer and nail to make two holes on the side
of the block of wood. Make the holes a little less than the
length of the paper clips. These holes will be pilot holes
for the screws. (Figure 13-1)

Make two small holes
for the screws.

They're called pilot
holes because they guide
the screws—just like a
pilot guides a plane.

Figure 13-1

YOU NEED

**Hammer and
small nail**

**Two wood or sheet
metal screws**

Two flat washers

Two paper clips

**Two bare copper
wires about 4 inches
(10 cm) long**

Wooden block

Screwdriver

**Test circuit such as
lights in series**

2   Place a washer on one of the screws, then thread the screw through the small end of one of the paper clips. Slide the remaining washer onto the screw next to the paper clip. (Figure 13-2)

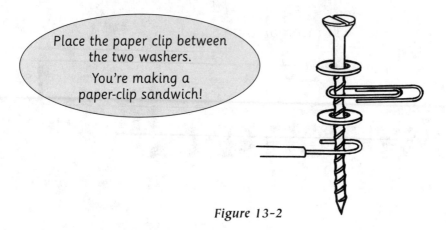

Place the paper clip between the two washers.

You're making a paper-clip sandwich!

Figure 13-2

3   Now make a small loop in the end of one of the wires and place it on the screw against the washer. Screw this assembly into one of the pilot holes. Tighten the screw enough so that the washer presses against the wire loop but still allows the paper clip to turn with slight pressure.

4   Insert the other screw through the small end of the other paper clip, and loop the remaining wire around the screw. (Figure 13-3)

Figure 13-3

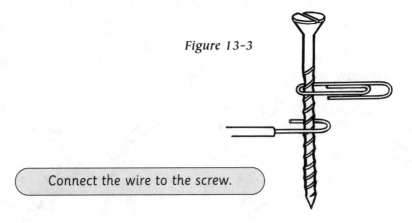

Connect the wire to the screw.

5 Install the screw inthe other pilot hole. Position the paper clip so that it stands straight up. Tighten this screw completely. You now should have one movable paper clip fastened by two flat washers that can slide into the clamp of the fixed paper clip. This will be the switch. A wire lead should be running from each screw. (Figure 13-4)

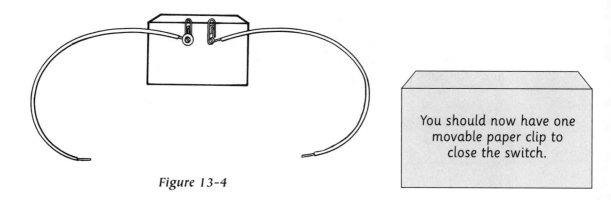

Figure 13-4

You should now have one movable paper clip to close the switch.

6 Connect the wire leads from the screws to a circuit and run a test. Did your switch work? (Figure 13-5)

Use a battery that matches the voltage of the bulbs.

If you did this right, it'll brighten your day!

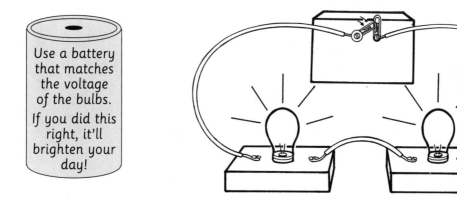

Figure 13-5

WHAT HAPPENED?

When you slide the movable paper clip into the clamp of the other paper clip, you are providing a path for an electrical current. The spring action of the fixed paper clip makes a good, reliable connection that can be used over and over again.

Switches can be mechanical or electronic. We all have wall switches in our homes to operate the lights, but where else would you find switches? What type of switches can you think of? How are streetlights turned on and off? Does a telephone use switches to dial a number?

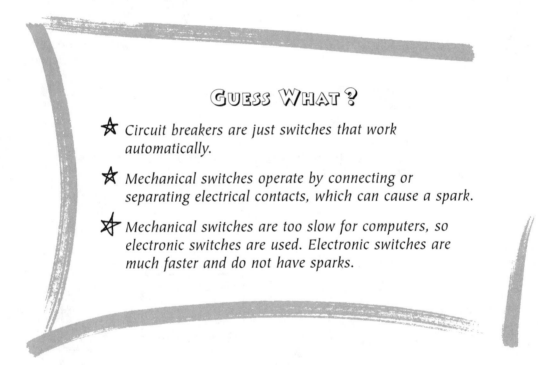

GUESS WHAT?

★ *Circuit breakers are just switches that work automatically.*

★ *Mechanical switches operate by connecting or separating electrical contacts, which can cause a spark.*

★ *Mechanical switches are too slow for computers, so electronic switches are used. Electronic switches are much faster and do not have sparks.*

Check it out!

CONDUCTORS AND INSULATORS

YOUR CHALLENGE

To investigate the difference between conductors and
insulators.

DO THIS

1 Have an adult carefully remove about 2 inches (5 cm) of
   insulation from the ends of each wire with the knife or
   clippers.

2 Use the screwdriver to loosen the terminal screws on the
   bulb holder.

3 Connect the bare end of two wires to the terminal screws
   on the bulb holder, and screw in the bulb.

4 Make a small coil in the bare end of one of the wires
   connected to the holder, and tape it to the bottom of the
   battery. Now make a similar coil in the unused wire, and

YOU NEED

Knife or nail clippers

**Three small insulated
copper wires about
7 inches (18 cm) long**

Small screwdriver

**Threaded-base
bulb holder**

**Threaded-base
flashlight bulb**

**Transparent or
masking tape**

D-cell battery

**Test materials found
around the home
such as a nail, knife
blade, spoon, paper,
glass, etc.**

tape it to the top of the battery for one lead. The other lead is connected to the bulb holder.

5   Touch the leads to the test material to see if it is a conductor or an insulator. How can you tell? (Figure 14-1)

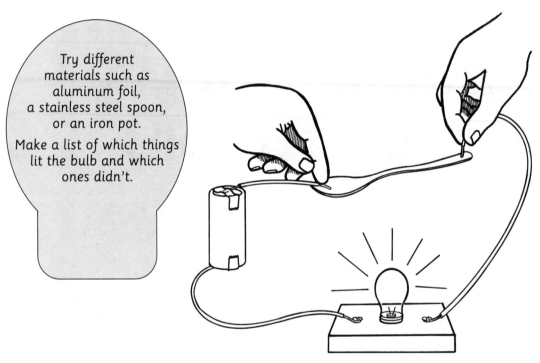

Try different materials such as aluminum foil, a stainless steel spoon, or an iron pot.

Make a list of which things lit the bulb and which ones didn't.

Figure 14-1

WHAT HAPPENED?

Materials can be divided into three basic classes: *conductors, semiconductors,* and *insulators*. The feature that creates these classes is the resistance of the material to the flow of electricity. The resistance is measured in *ohms*. Most metals, such as gold, copper, and aluminum, are good conductors, while insulators are poor conductors. Semiconductors fall somewhere in between. A transistor is a semiconductor.

Do you think tap water is a good conductor of electricity? How about distilled water? What other conductors or insulators can you think of? Would an insulator resist the flow of heat as well as electricity?

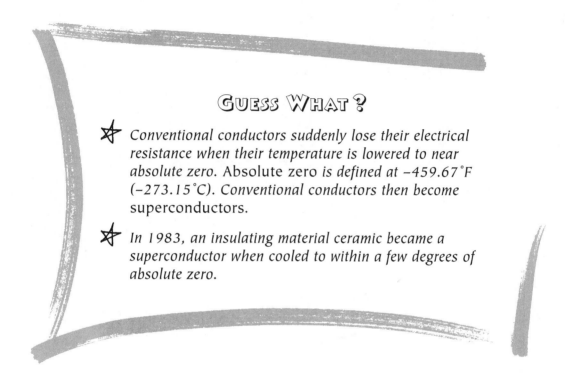

GUESS WHAT?

★ Conventional conductors suddenly lose their electrical resistance when their temperature is lowered to near absolute zero. Absolute zero is defined at –459.67°F (–273.15°C). Conventional conductors then become superconductors.

★ In 1983, an insulating material ceramic became a superconductor when cooled to within a few degrees of absolute zero.

60

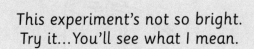

This experiment's not so bright.
Try it...You'll see what I mean.

SLOW THE FLOW

YOUR CHALLENGE

To observe how some materials can be used to vary the flow of electricity.

DO THIS

1 Connect one end of the wire to the top of the battery and fasten it in place with tape. (Figure 15-1)

YOU NEED

Uninsulated copper wire

D-cell battery

Transparent tape

Full length of pencil lead from mechanical pencil

Flashlight bulb

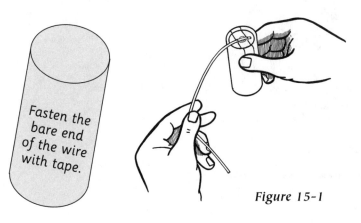

Fasten the bare end of the wire with tape.

Figure 15-1

2   Twist the other end of the wire tightly around the metal side of the bulb. (Figure 15-2)

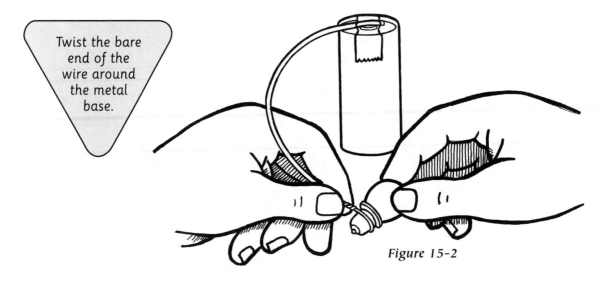

Twist the bare end of the wire around the metal base.

Figure 15-2

3   Place the pencil lead on a flat surface, and rest the bottom of the battery on one end of the lead. (Figure 15-3)

Touch the metal point on the bottom of the bulb to the lead.

Did you know that pencil lead isn't lead? It's carbon!

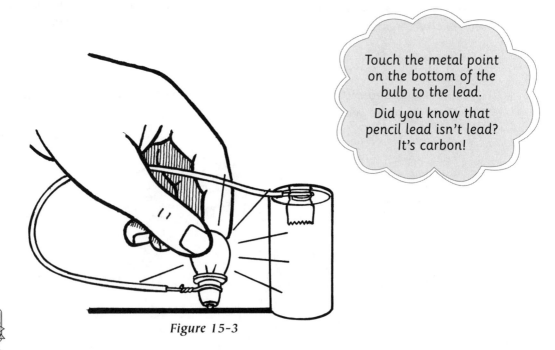

Figure 15-3

4 Now touch the bottom of the bulb to the lead close to the battery. Notice the brightness of the bulb. Gradually slide the bulb down the length of the lead. What do you see? (Figure 15-4)

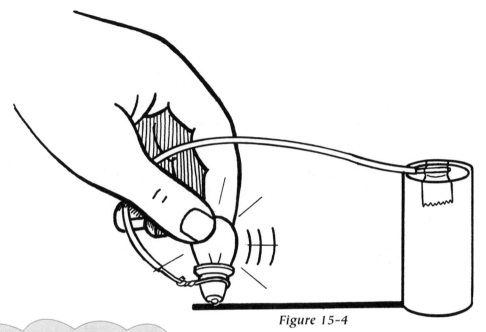

Figure 15-4

Slide the bulb farther away from the battery.

What happens to the bulb?

WHAT HAPPENED?

As the bulb moves along the lead, the resistance of the lead between the bulb and the battery increases. The pencil lead becomes a *rheostat*, which is a kind of resistor used to control current.

Where would rheostats be useful? Is a light-dimming switch a type of rheostat? What is a *potentiometer*? Can it control the flow of electricity? Is a volume control a potentiometer? How would you control the speed of an electric motor?

63

GUESS WHAT?

⭐ Before the 1920s, factories used machines connected to one central steam engine or large motor. The motor drove a network of shafts and pulleys connected to leather belts that supplied power to each machine. These factories were noisy and dangerous workplaces.

⭐ About half of today's electric generating plants are coal-fired.

Will there be light?

FUSE NEWS

YOUR CHALLENGE

To build a device to test fuses.

DO THIS

1   Separate the two sections of an old lamp cord for the wires. (Figure 16-1)

 2   Cut the wires to the lengths needed to make three wires. Have an adult strip about 1 inch (2.5 cm) of the insulation from the ends of the wires with the knife or clippers.

3   Twist the bare ends to keep the strands together. (Figure 16-2)

4   Tape one end of the short wire to one end of the battery, and connect the other end of the wire to a screw on the bulb holder.

Two insulated wires about 16 inches (40 cm) long

One insulated wire about 3 inches (8 cm) long

Knife or nail clippers

Transparent tape

Threaded-base bulb holder

1.5-volt flashlight battery

Flashlight bulb

Fuses to be tested

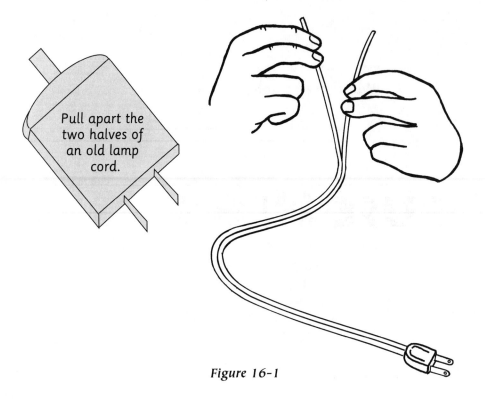

Pull apart the two halves of an old lamp cord.

Figure 16-1

Figure 16-2

Twist the ends to keep the strands together.

Those ends are sharp!

5   Connect the end of one of the longer wires to the other screw on the bulb holder.

6   Now tape the bulb holder to the side of the battery.

7   Tape the remaining long wire to the other end of the battery. The free ends of the long wires are the leads for the tester.

8   Touch the leads to each end of a fuse. What happens? Is the fuse good or bad? How do you know? (Figures 16-3 and 16-4)

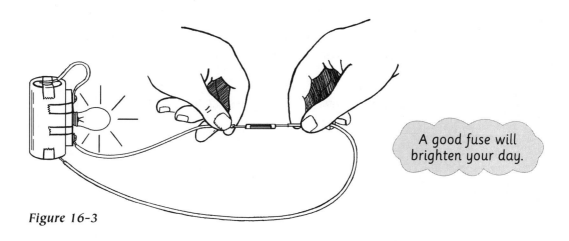

A good fuse will brighten your day.

Figure 16-3

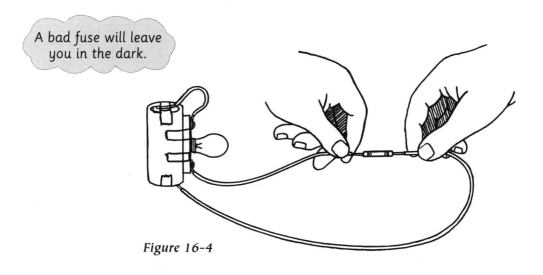

A bad fuse will leave you in the dark.

Figure 16-4

WHAT HAPPENED?

The good fuse caused the lightbulb to light. The bad fuse did not. If you find a bad fuse, does this mean that something is wrong in the circuit? Before replacing the fuse, should the circuit be checked?

GUESS WHAT?

★ Homes in the United States use about one-third of the electrical power produced in the world.

★ A car's electrical system provides only 12 volts, but the ignition system's coil can deliver up to 30,000 volts to the spark plugs.

Bet you'll really be attracted to this experiment!

MAGNIFICENT MAGNETS

YOUR CHALLENGE

To observe the behavior of a magnet.

DO THIS

1   Hold the magnet against the nail and bring one end of the nail to the paper clips. What happens? (Figure 17-1)

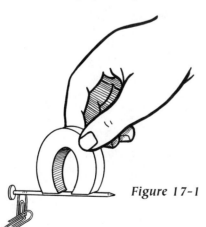

Figure 17-1

The nail is magnetized. See who can pick up the most paper clips. You'll need a steady hand!

2   Remove the magnet from the nail. Now what happens to the paper clips? (Figure 17-2)

Figure 17-2

⚠ 3   Stroke the needle about 20 times with one end of the magnet. (Figure 17-3)

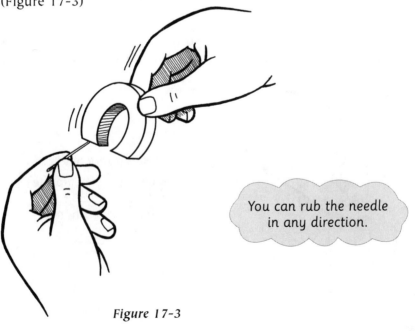

Figure 17-3

4 Set the magnet aside, and try using just the needle to pick up the paper clips. Does this work? (Figure 17-4)

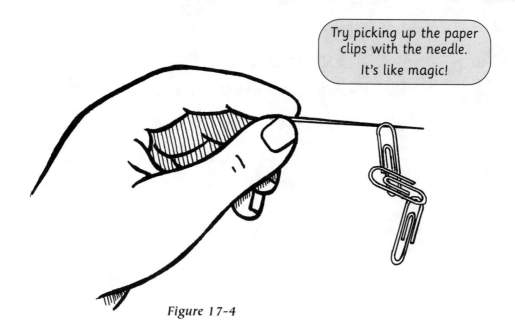

Try picking up the paper clips with the needle.

It's like magic!

Figure 17-4

WHAT HAPPENED?

When the magnet is touching the nail, the *magnetic field* aligned all of the atoms in the nail in the same direction. As long as the magnet is touching the nail, the nail could pick up the paper clips. But because the nail is made of iron, a softer metal, most of the atoms returned to their jumbled state when the magnet is removed. The nail lost almost all of its magnetism.

The needle is made of steel, and steel is very hard. It is harder to magnetize. Steel keeps its magnetic field a lot longer, so the needle itself can pick up the paper clips.

Where can you find magnets around the home? Could magnets be used to keep cabinet doors closed? Could magnets be used to keep things apart or to separate certain materials? Do some types of locks and alarms use magnets?

71

GUESS WHAT?

★ Even a doorbell won't work without magnetism.

★ Light itself is part electrical and part magnetic.

Feeling Lost?
This experiment could help
you find your way around!

CONSTRUCT A COMPASS!

YOUR CHALLENGE

To make a magnetic compass.

DO THIS

1 Fold the paper in the middle to make a 1-inch square (2.5 cm).

 2 Thread the needle and tie a knot on the end of the thread so it won't pull through the hole.

3 Spread the paper a little and push the needle through the center from the inside of the fold. Gently pull the needle through the paper so that the knot is not pulled through. (Figure 18-1)

Carefully pull the thread up to the knot.

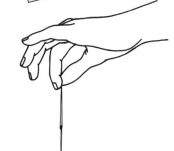

Figure 18-1

YOU NEED

Strip of paper about 1 x 2 inches (2.5 x 5 cm)

Steel needle

Fine thread about 8 inches (20 cm) long

Wooden pencil

Clear drinking glass

Magnet

4 Remove the thread from the needle, and tie the free end around the middle of the pencil. The length of the thread should suspend the paper about 1 inch (2.5 cm) or so above the bottom of the glass. (Figure 18-2)

Tie the thread to the pencil.

Make sure the paper doesn't touch the bottom of the glass.

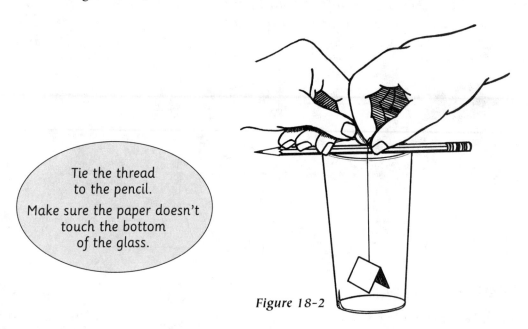

Figure 18-2

5 Magnetize the needle by stroking it about 20 times with one end of the magnet. (Figure 18-3)

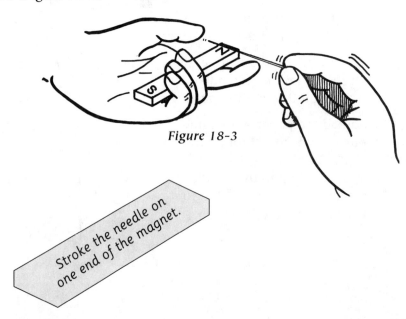

Figure 18-3

Stroke the needle on one end of the magnet.

6 Now with the paper spread tent-like, insert the needle horizontally through both sides of the paper. Center the needle so that it will balance. (Figure 18-4)

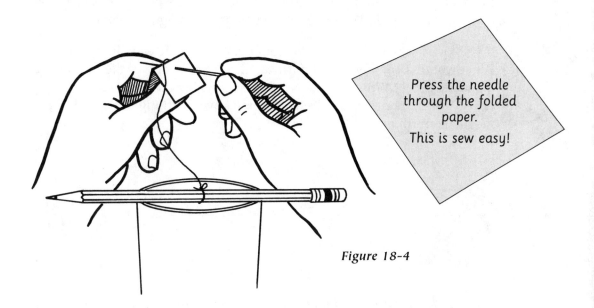

Press the needle through the folded paper.

This is sew easy!

Figure 18-4

7 Lower the needle inside the glass so that it is suspended freely by the thread and the pencil. Watch the needle carefully. What does it do? (Figure 18-5)

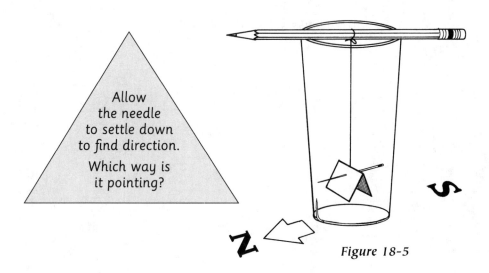

Allow the needle to settle down to find direction.

Which way is it pointing?

Figure 18-5

WHAT HAPPENED?

The earth has a huge magnetic field, with the magnetic north pole near the geographic north pole. One end of the needle is pointing *magnetic north*, not *true north*. Why does the earth have a magnetic field?

If you know which way is north, could you find your way in the woods? What would a compass read if it was directly over one of the earth's magnetic poles? What are the Northern Lights, or the *aurora borealis* (uh-ROAR-uh boor-ree-AL-liss)? Do they have anything to do with the magnetic north pole?

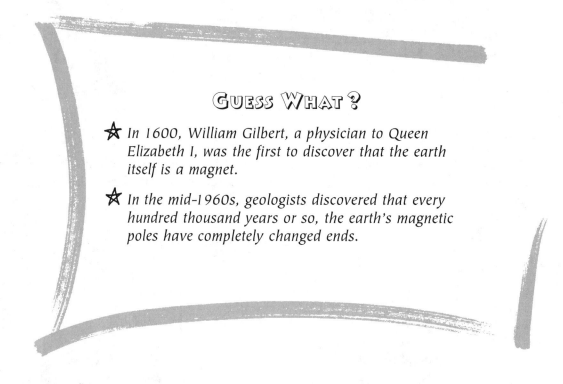

GUESS WHAT?

★ In 1600, William Gilbert, a physician to Queen Elizabeth I, was the first to discover that the earth itself is a magnet.

★ In the mid-1960s, geologists discovered that every hundred thousand years or so, the earth's magnetic poles have completely changed ends.

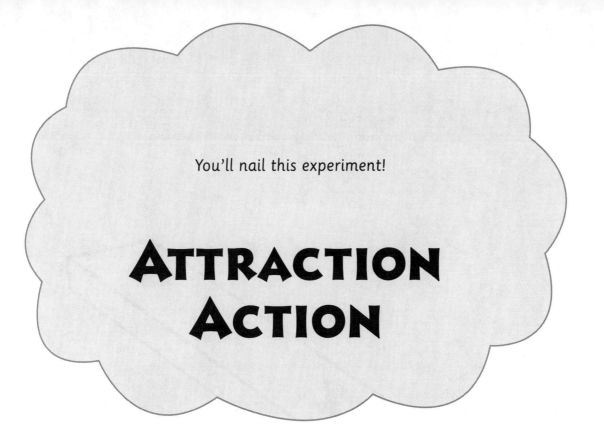

You'll nail this experiment!

ATTRACTION ACTION

YOUR CHALLENGE

To investigate how a magnet may both attract and repel objects.

DO THIS

1 Using one end of the magnet, attach the nails, end-to-end, to the magnet. (Figure 19-1)

2 The magnetic field of the magnet produced a magnetic field in each nail because the first nail was exposed to the magnetic force of the magnet. Then the second nail, the third, and so on. The process is called magnetic induction.

Magnet

Nails

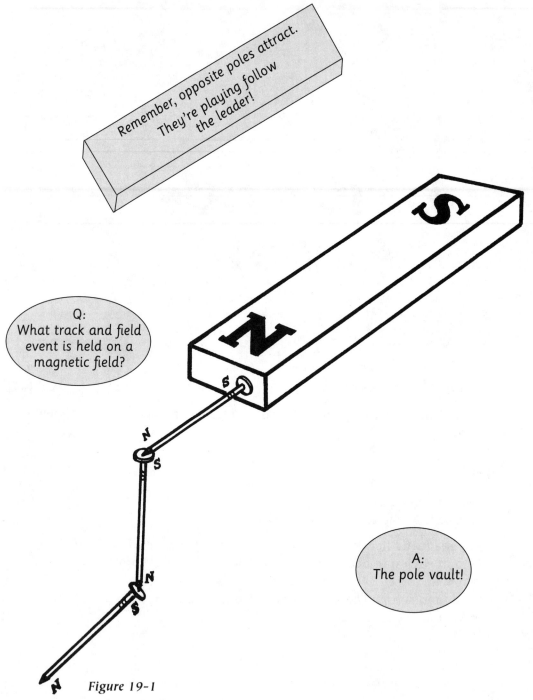

Figure 19-1

What Happened?

Because unlike *poles* (the ends of a magnet or battery) attract, if you used the "north" pole of the magnet, the "south" pole of the nail will touch the magnet, and the other end of the nail will be the "north" pole. This means that even if several nails are used, the free end of the last nail will have the same *polarity* as the pole that was used on the magnet.

When using a compass, what is the polarity of the end of the needle that points north? What animals can you think of that might use the earth's magnetic field? How do bees find their way back to the hive?

Guess What?

★ Marine life such as rays and sharks, as well as migrating birds, can sense and use the earth's magnetic field. Migrating birds use it for navigating, while some fish use electrical and magnetic disturbances to detect live food sources.

★ Researchers believe that strong magnetic fields can be a health hazard. Strong magnetic fields can interfere with the normal functions of our bodies, which are all controlled by small electrical signals.

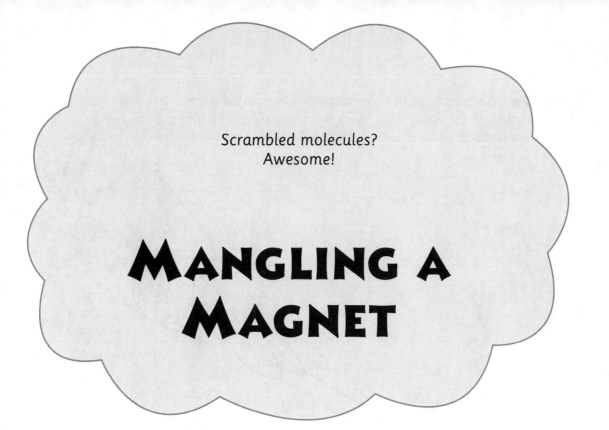

Scrambled molecules?
Awesome!

MANGLING A
MAGNET

YOUR CHALLENGE

To explore the conditions that would cause a magnet to lose its magnetism.

DO THIS

 1 Place one of the saw blades on a hard surface and strike it several times with the hammer. (Figure 20-1)

YOU NEED

Two magnetized hacksaw blades

Hot stove or candle

Hammer

Tongs or pliers

Nail or paper clips

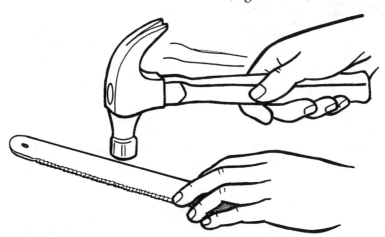

Figure 20-1

81

2 Have your adult partner use tongs or pliers to heat the other saw blade over the stove. (If a stove is unavailable, a candle may be used.) (Figure 20-2)

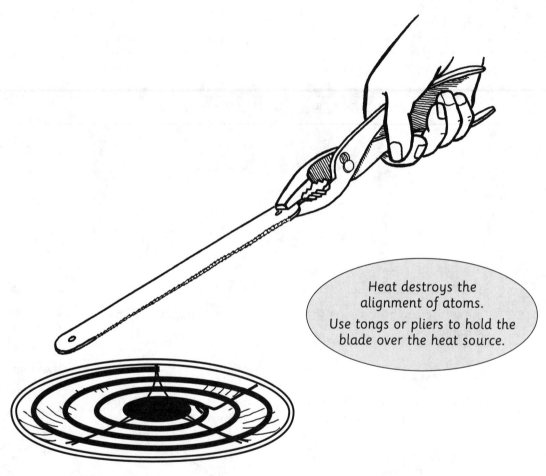

Heat destroys the alignment of atoms.

Use tongs or pliers to hold the blade over the heat source.

Figure 20-2

3 Try to pick up a paper clip with the first saw blade.

4 When cooled, try to pick up a paper clip with the other saw blade. What happens?

82

WHAT HAPPENED?

The atoms in a magnet are aligned in the same direction. Hitting or heating will jumble the atoms. The atoms lose their alignment, and the magnetic field disappears. (Figure 20-3)

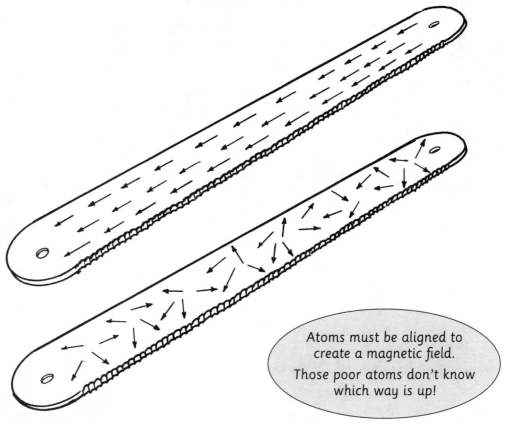

Atoms must be aligned to create a magnetic field.

Those poor atoms don't know which way is up!

Figure 20-3

If heat destroys a magnet, how do you think freezing will affect it? Would you expect to find magnets on space shuttles or satellites in orbit? Why or why not? How far in space do you think the earth's magnetic field goes? Is there any connection between gravity and magnetism?

GUESS WHAT ?

★ *No one has been able to separate the poles of a magnet. If you kept on cutting the magnet in half, each piece will still have two poles.*

★ *By 1980, high-speed trains floating on a magnetic field could travel up to 300 miles per hour.*

Just follow this magnetic map to the north and south poles!

MAGNETIC MAPPING

YOUR CHALLENGE

To follow the paths of a magnetic field from one pole to the other.

DO THIS

1 Bring the compass near the "south" pole of the magnet. What happens? (Figure 21-1)

YOU NEED

Compass

Magnet

Figure 21-1

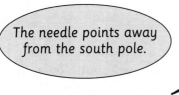

The needle points away from the south pole.

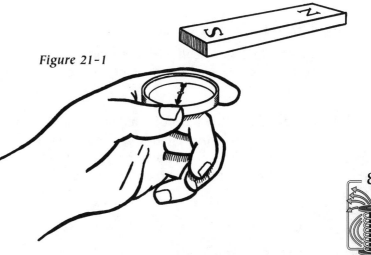

2 Now slowly move the compass in the direction of the needle. What happens? (Figure 21-2)

> The needle follows the line of force of the magnetic field.
> You're playing Follow-the-Needle!

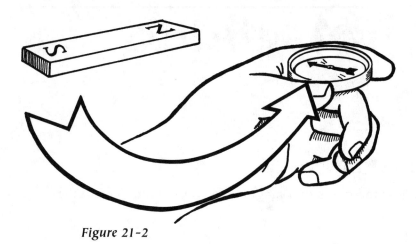

Figure 21-2

WHAT HAPPENED?

The needle aligns itself with the magnetic field. By following the needle, the compass traveled the lines of force of the magnetic field between the two poles.

You found that the lines of a magnetic field pointed down into the poles of a magnet. Would this mean that a compass on its side would point down at the earth's magnetic north pole? Would it point up at the magnetic south pole? Where would it point on the equator?

GUESS WHAT?

★ *Magnetic traps are often used in food processing to protect the food from metal contaminants.*

★ *Magnets are installed on some yard vehicles to pick up hazardous nails and scrap metal.*

88

You can mess up a magnet
if you do this one right!

POT LUCK

YOUR CHALLENGE

To investigate the effects of aluminum and steel on magnetic fields.

DO THIS

1   Lower the compass into the aluminum pot and watch the needle. What does it do? (Figure 22-1)

YOU NEED

Compass (with a suspended magnetized needle)

Aluminum pot

Iron pot

Wooden bowl (optional)

Glass bowl (optional)

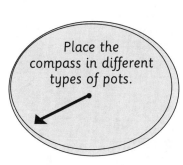

Place the compass in different types of pots.

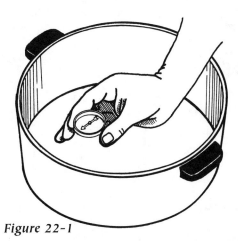

Figure 22-1

2   Now try the iron pot. What happens to the needle?

WHAT HAPPENED?

Inside the iron pot, the needle may point in any direction or could even swing back and forth. The earth's magnetic lines did not pass through the iron pot.

Place the compass inside a wooden bowl, then try a glass one. Does the compass still work? When ships were made of wood, magnetic compasses worked fine. What is a *gyrocompass*? Why do you think ships today use them?

GUESS WHAT?

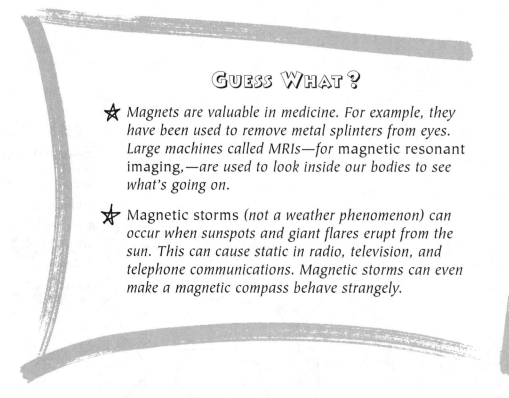

⭐ *Magnets are valuable in medicine. For example, they have been used to remove metal splinters from eyes. Large machines called MRIs—for magnetic resonant imaging,—are used to look inside our bodies to see what's going on.*

⭐ *Magnetic storms (not a weather phenomenon) can occur when sunspots and giant flares erupt from the sun. This can cause static in radio, television, and telephone communications. Magnetic storms can even make a magnetic compass behave strangely.*

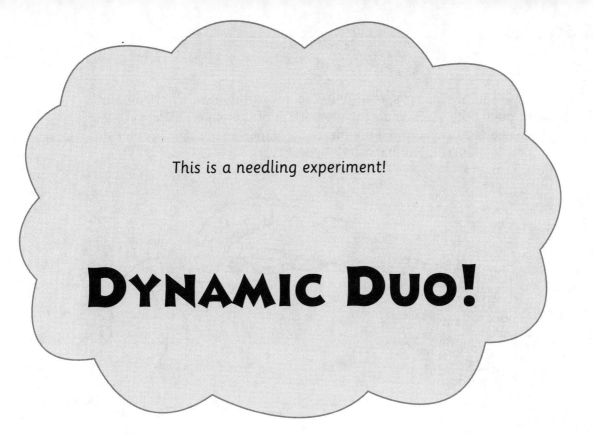

This is a needling experiment!

DYNAMIC DUO!

YOUR CHALLENGE

To investigate the effect an electrical current has on a magnetic field.

DO THIS

 1 Fold the paper in the middle to make a 1-inch square (2.5 cm). Thread the needle and tie a knot on the end of the thread so it won't pull through the hole.

2 Spread the paper a little and push the needle through the center from the inside of the fold. Gently pull the needle through the paper so that the knot is not pulled through. Remove the thread from the needle.

 3 Magnetize the needle by stroking it about 20 times with one end of the magnet.

YOU NEED

Piece of paper about 1 x 2 inches (2.5 x 5 cm)

Steel needle

Fine thread about 8 inches (20 cm) long

Magnet

Lamp

4 Now with the paper spread tent-like, insert the needle horizontally through both sides and near the bottom of the paper. Make sure the needle is as close to the bottom of the paper as possible. Center the needle so that it will balance. (Figure 23-1)

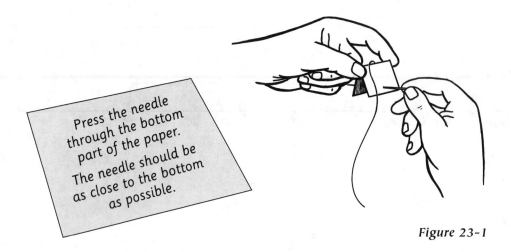

Press the needle through the bottom part of the paper. The needle should be as close to the bottom as possible.

Figure 23-1

 5 Turn on the electric lamp and place a section of the lamp cord on a flat surface.

6 Hold the end of the thread and allow the needle to settle down. It will align itself north and south. This is a simple compass. (Figure 23-2)

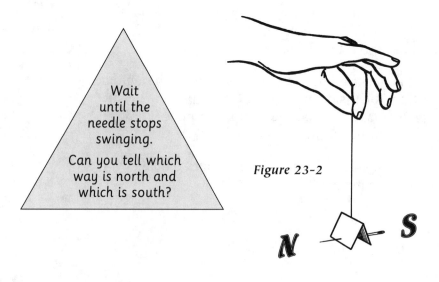

Wait until the needle stops swinging.

Can you tell which way is north and which is south?

Figure 23-2

7   Run the lamp cord east and west and slowly lower the needle over the cord. What happens when the needle gets near the cord? Can you explain what you see? (Figure 23-3)

Figure 23-3

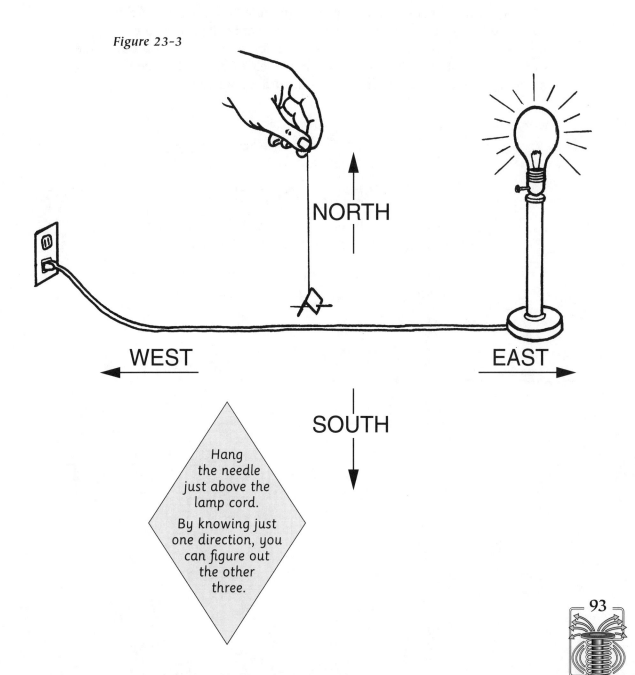

NORTH

WEST

EAST

SOUTH

Hang the needle just above the lamp cord.

By knowing just one direction, you can figure out the other three.

WHAT HAPPENED?

The flow of an electrical current will have a magnetic field of its own and will affect the magnetic field of a compass.

Other than the earth's magnetic field, think of all the magnetic fields surrounding us from powerlines and electric cables in our schools and homes. Tune a portable radio to an AM station and walk near a powerline. Can you hear static, indicating a magnetic field? Could the magnetic fields along high-voltage transmission lines in rural areas be useful? How?

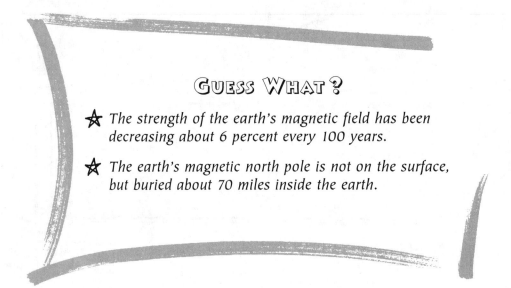

GUESS WHAT?

★ *The strength of the earth's magnetic field has been decreasing about 6 percent every 100 years.*

★ *The earth's magnetic north pole is not on the surface, but buried about 70 miles inside the earth.*

Here's a shocking way to
make a magnet!

ELECTRO MAGIC!

YOUR CHALLENGE

To generate a magnetic field using an electrical current.

DO THIS

1 Place one of the washers on the bolt. Leave a few inches of wire for a lead. (Figure 24-1)

2 Traveling up the length of the bolt, wrap the wire about 50 times around the bolt. (Figure 24-2)

3 Leave a little wire at the end for another lead, and slide the other washer over the bolt. Screw the nut in place. (Figure 24-3)

 4 Have an adult carefully trim about an inch (2.5 cm) of insulation off each end of the wire with the knife or clippers.

YOU NEED

Iron bolt about 3 inches (8 cm) long

One nut and two washers to fit bolt

Small insulated copper wire about 3 feet (1 m) long

Knife or nail clippers

Lantern battery

Paper clips, small nails, etc.

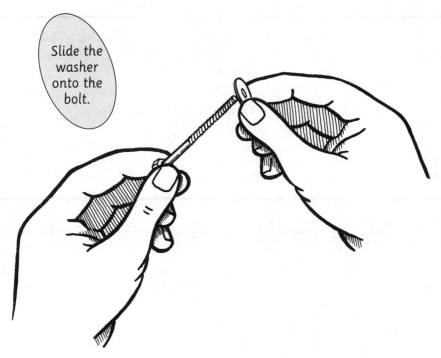

Slide the washer onto the bolt.

Figure 24-1

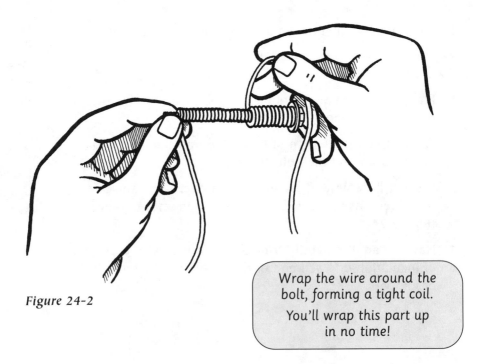

Figure 24-2

Wrap the wire around the bolt, forming a tight coil.

You'll wrap this part up in no time!

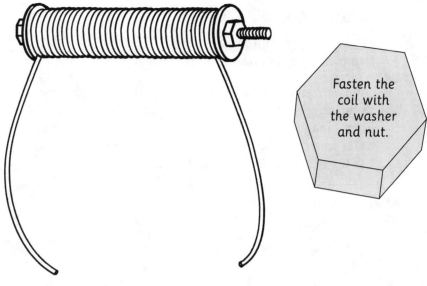

Fasten the coil with the washer and nut.

Figure 24-3

5   Attach one of the wire leads to the positive terminal of a battery and the other lead to the negative terminal. This is an electromagnet. How can you test its magnetic properties? (Figure 24-4)

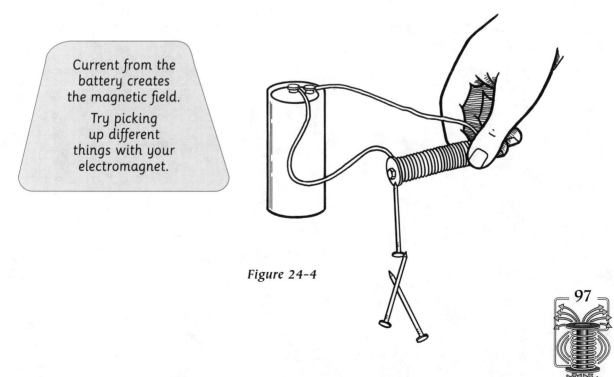

Current from the battery creates the magnetic field.

Try picking up different things with your electromagnet.

Figure 24-4

WHAT HAPPENED?

When the ends of the coil are connected to a battery, the electromagnet can pick up small nails and paper clips.

An electromagnet called a *solenoid* (SO-la-noyd) operates the starting motor that starts the engine in a car. Can you think of any other uses for electromagnets or solenoids? How do you think electric valves that turn lawn sprinklers on and off work? How does an icemaker in a refrigerator get water? How does an electric lock work?

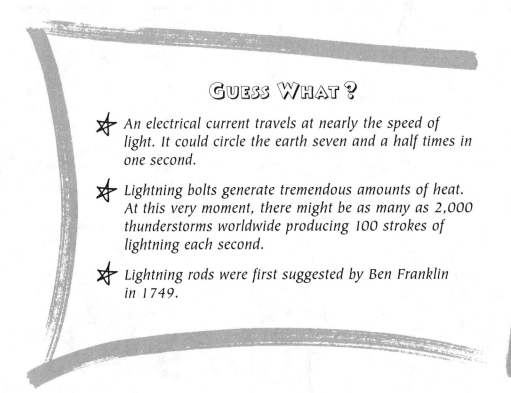

GUESS WHAT?

⭐ *An electrical current travels at nearly the speed of light. It could circle the earth seven and a half times in one second.*

⭐ *Lightning bolts generate tremendous amounts of heat. At this very moment, there might be as many as 2,000 thunderstorms worldwide producing 100 strokes of lightning each second.*

⭐ *Lightning rods were first suggested by Ben Franklin in 1749.*

How can you measure something you can't see? This experiment will show you!

GREAT GALVANOMETER!

YOUR CHALLENGE

To build a meter that will detect an electrical current.

DO THIS

1 Fold two ends of the cardboard up to form supports for the wire, then wrap the wire around the cardboard about 30 times. Leave about 12 inches (30 cm) of extra wire for connections. (Figure 25-1)

Wrap the wire around the cardboard base.

Don't forget to leave extra wire at the ends.

YOU NEED

3 x 4-inch (7.5 x 10 cm) piece of cardboard

Insulated wire (bell wire)

Knife or nail clippers

Compass

Flashlight battery

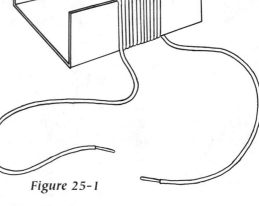

Figure 25-1

99

2   Have an adult strip about 1/2 inch (1.5 cm) of the insulation from each end of the wire with the knife or clippers.

3   Place the compass on the cardboard and beneath the wire. Turn the cardboard so that the wires run east and west. (Figure 25-2)

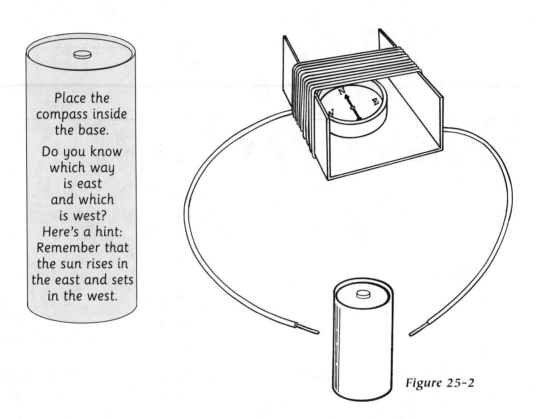

Place the compass inside the base.

Do you know which way is east and which is west? Here's a hint: Remember that the sun rises in the east and sets in the west.

Figure 25-2

4   Connect the wires to the battery. What happens to the needle? What does this tell you? (Figure 25-3)

WHAT HAPPENED?

You have constructed a galvanometer. A *galvanometer* is a meter that can detect very small amounts of current and voltage. The galvanometer you created uses a magnetic field to sense current and voltage.

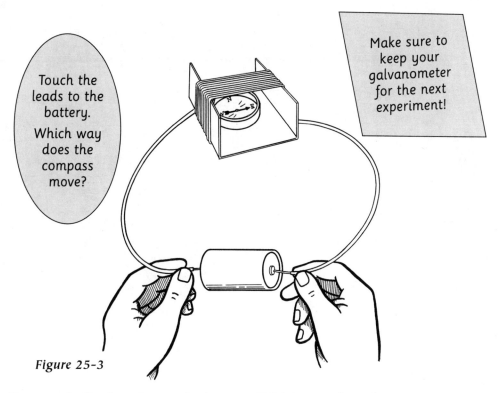

Touch the leads to the battery.

Which way does the compass move?

Make sure to keep your galvanometer for the next experiment!

Figure 25-3

Reverse the leads going to the battery. Which way does the compass needle move now? Does this mean that the direction the current is flowing affects the magnetic field?

As you read, small electric currents are speeding along nerves from your eyes to your brain. How much voltage would you guess that our bodies carry? What is a *millivolt*?

GUESS WHAT?

★ *Electricity has no weight, color, size, or odor. Nobody knows fully what electricity is, only that it is a basic object of nature.*

You can generate some interest when you do this experiment—not to mention electricity!

CURRENT EVENTS

YOUR CHALLENGE

To produce an electrical current from a magnetic field.

DO THIS

1   Wrap the wire around your fingers about 30 times to make a coil. It should be a little larger than the bar magnet. Leave a length free at each end to make connections. (Figure 26-1)

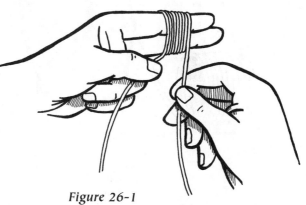

Use your fingers to form a coil.

Don't wrap too tightly or your fingers will turn purple!

Figure 26-1

YOU NEED

Insulated wire (bell wire)

Knife or nail clippers

Bar magnet

Galvanometer (see preceding experiment)

103

2 Have an adult carefully remove about ½ inch (1.5 cm) of the insulation on each end with the knife or clippers.

3 Connect the ends of the wire to the galvanometer constructed in the previous experiment. (Figure 26-2)

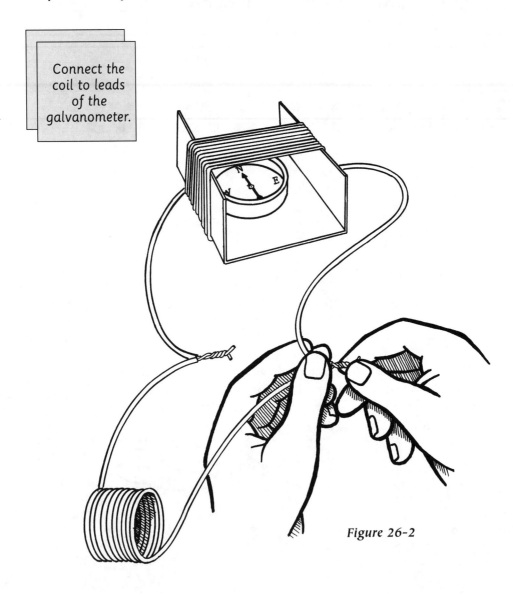

Connect the coil to leads of the galvanometer.

Figure 26-2

4 Move the bar magnet abruptly in and out of the center of the coil. Notice the direction of the movement of the needle. Can you explain this? (Figure 26-3)

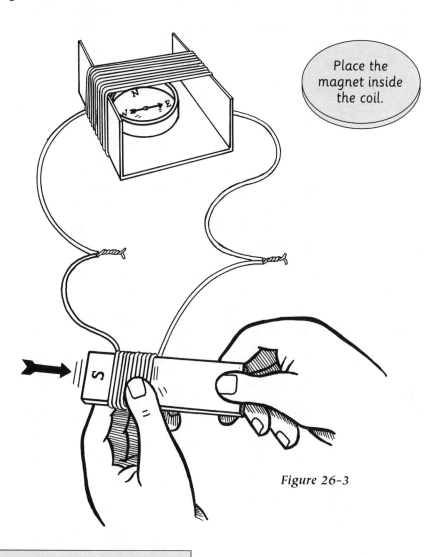

Place the magnet inside the coil.

Figure 26-3

Rapidly move the magnet in and out of the coil.

Now you see it; now you don't.

WHAT HAPPENED?

How do you think the current could be increased? What would happen if you added more loops in the coil? What is a *generator*? How does it work? If the current reverses, is this *alternating current* (AC)?

GUESS WHAT?

★ Artificial arms and hands can be controlled by built-in connectors that pick up nerve signals from the wearer's muscles. The signals are converted into an electric current and sent to tiny motors that operate the arm-hand unit.

★ An electric generator works the same way as an electric motor except in reverse. A generator changes mechanical energy into electrical energy, while a motor changes electrical energy into mechanical energy.

This one could make
you loopy if you let it!

LOOPY LOOPS

YOUR CHALLENGE

To compare the ability of a magnet to produce an electrical current in a closed and open loop of wire.

DO THIS

 1 The loops should be about 4 to 5 inches (10 to 12 cm) across. Spread the ends of one of the loops so that there is a small gap. Twist the ends of the other loop together, or have an adult solder (SOD-der) them. This makes one open loop and one closed loop.

2 Suspend each loop by two strings from a support, such as a ruler across two books. (Figure 27-1)

3 Insert one end of the magnet into the open loop and watch the movement of the loop. What do you see? (Figure 27-2)

YOU NEED

Two heavy, bare copper wire loops (12-gauge or larger)

String

Table

Two rulers and two stacks of books, or other items, for support

Strong bar magnet

Soldering iron and solder (optional)

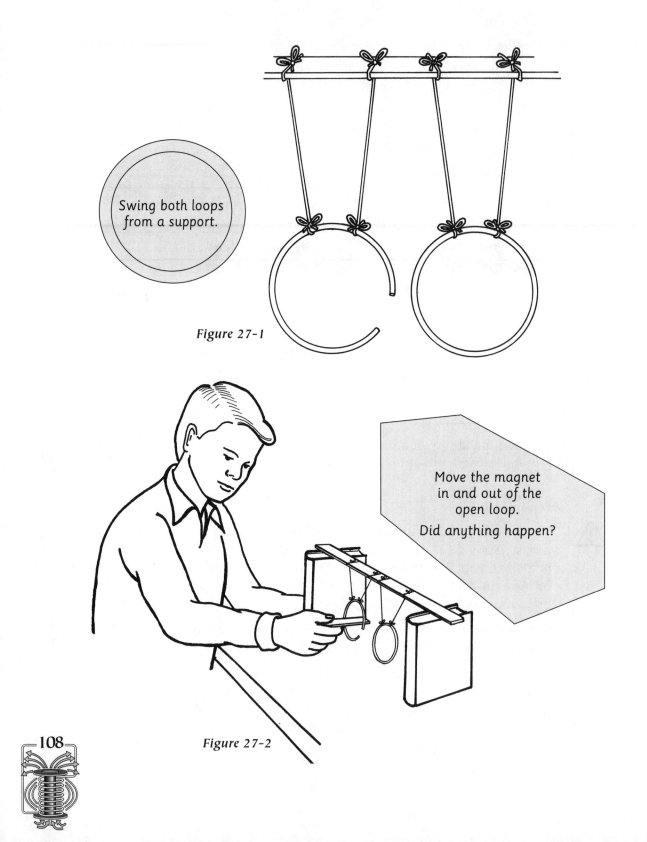

Swing both loops from a support.

Figure 27-1

Move the magnet in and out of the open loop.

Did anything happen?

Figure 27-2

4 Next, insert the magnet into the closed loop. Now what do you see? Can you explain what happened? (Figure 27-3)

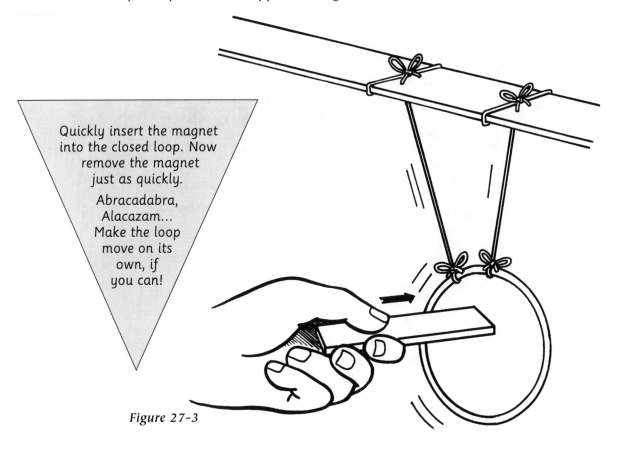

Quickly insert the magnet into the closed loop. Now remove the magnet just as quickly.

Abracadabra, Alacazam... Make the loop move on its own, if you can!

Figure 27-3

WHAT HAPPENED?

The magnetic field of the magnet induced, or brought about, an electrical current in the closed loop. This current produced its own magnetic field, which was repelled and attracted to the magnet. No current flowed in the open loop because there must be a continuous path for current to flow.

A larger-diameter wire carries more current than a smaller-diameter wire. Do you think a smaller wire would carry more current if it was wound into several loops? Would a stronger magnet produce more current? What type of machine uses this principle?

GUESS WHAT?

★ *In the United States, generating plants provide alternating current (AC) that reverses the direction of flow and changes polarity 60 times every second.*

★ *Electricity is the chief source of power in the United States.*

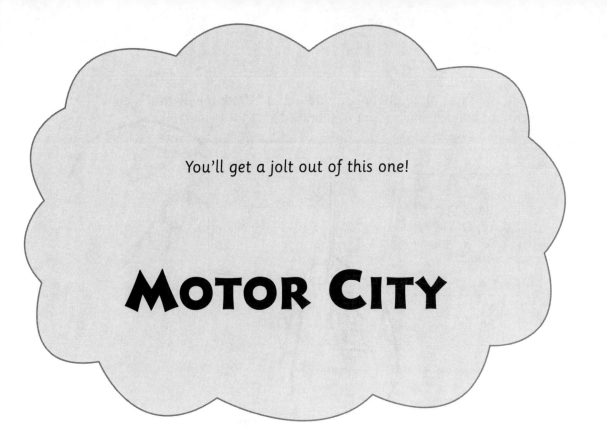

You'll get a jolt out of this one!

MOTOR CITY

YOUR CHALLENGE

To investigate how a magnetic field makes a motor turn.

DO THIS

1   Fold the ends of the cardboard up to make a support for the pencil, then press the pencil through each side of the cardboard folds near the top. (Figure 28-1)

Press the pencil through the cardboard base.

You might want to cut X's in the cardboard first so that the pencil pokes through easily.

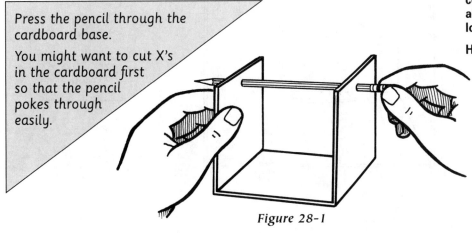

Figure 28-1

YOU NEED

Cardboard support

Pencil

Short piece of solid copper or aluminum wire

Flashlight battery

Two lengths of small copper wire each about 2 feet (60 cm) long

Horseshoe magnet

111

2 Bend the short piece of copper wire into a "U" shape, with the ends bent out about ¼ inch (5 mm). (Figure 28-2)

Bend the copper wire into the shape of a "U".

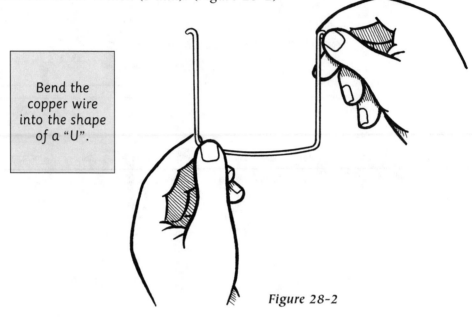

Figure 28-2

3 Now tie one end of one of the small copper wires tightly to the bend in the solid copper or aluminum wire. Connect the end of the other copper wire to the other bend the same way.

4 Loop the wires over the pencil a couple of times so that the copper "U" is suspended from the pencil like a swing. (Figure 28-3)

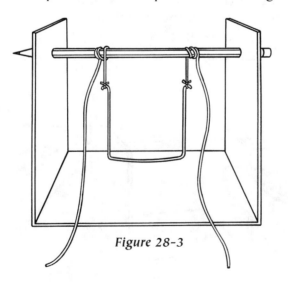

Figure 28-3

The "U" should be suspended from the pencil like a swing.

5   Position the horseshoe magnet on its side so that the copper "U" is free to swing between the poles of the magnet.

6   Connect the ends of the small copper wire to the battery. What happens when you do this? (Figure 28-4)

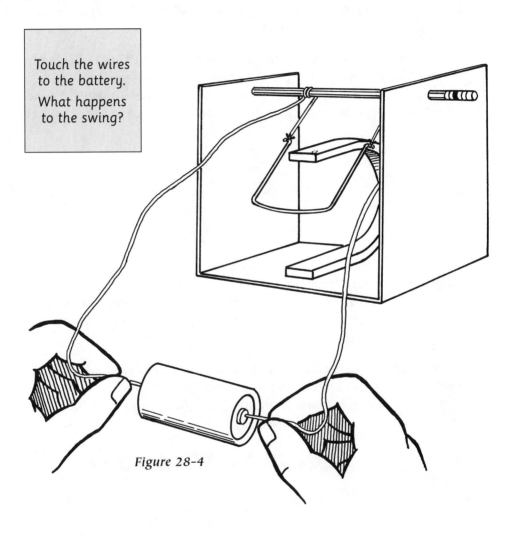

Touch the wires to the battery.

What happens to the swing?

Figure 28-4

7   Now swap the ends of the battery. What do you see? Can you explain what happened?

WHAT HAPPENED?

The copper "U" will swing out or in, depending on which way the current flows. Swapping the ends of the battery changed the direction of the current. When the current flows through the copper "U," it becomes an electromagnet, and it is attracted or repelled from the magnet. This is the principle that makes a motor operate.

Because a battery was used, the motor would be a DC (*direct current*) motor. Where could you find DC motors in use? Do you think an AC (*alternating current*) or a DC motor is used to operate windshield wipers on a car? What type of motor would you find in an electric car or golf cart?

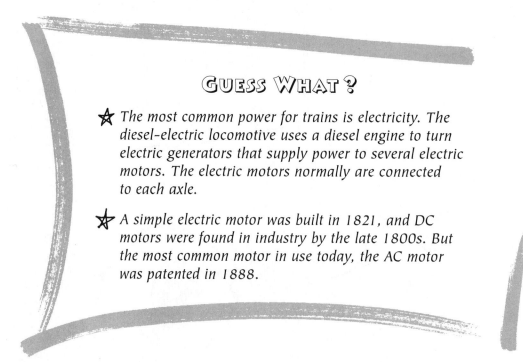

GUESS WHAT?

★ *The most common power for trains is electricity. The diesel-electric locomotive uses a diesel engine to turn electric generators that supply power to several electric motors. The electric motors normally are connected to each axle.*

★ *A simple electric motor was built in 1821, and DC motors were found in industry by the late 1800s. But the most common motor in use today, the AC motor was patented in 1888.*

You'll flip for this experiment!

MAKE A MOTOR!

YOUR CHALLENGE

To build a simple DC electric motor.

DO THIS

 1 Drive the two nails partway into the block of wood about 1½ inches (4 cm) apart. Leave about 1 inch (2.5 cm) of each nail sticking up.

 2 Cut the 22-gauge copper in half. Using the sandpaper, scrape the varnish from the ends of each wire. You'll need at least 1 inch (2.5 cm) of bare wire on each end.

3 Now use the pencil to form a small loop in one end of each wire. Make a similar loop in one end of the other wire. (Figure 29-1)

4 Wrap one of the wires around one of the nails about five times, leaving the loop sticking straight up from the nail about 2 inches (5 cm).

YOU NEED

Hammer

Two small nails about 1½ inches (4 cm) long

Block of wood for base

Varnished copper wire, about 22-gauge and 24 inches (60 cm) long

Wire cutters or heavy scissors

Sandpaper

Pencil

Varnished copper wire, about 26-gauge and 18 inches (50 cm) long

Large felt-tip marker, wooden dowel, or large pen about ½ inch (1.5 cm) in diameter

Two D-cell batteries

Holder with leads for batteries

Small magnet

115

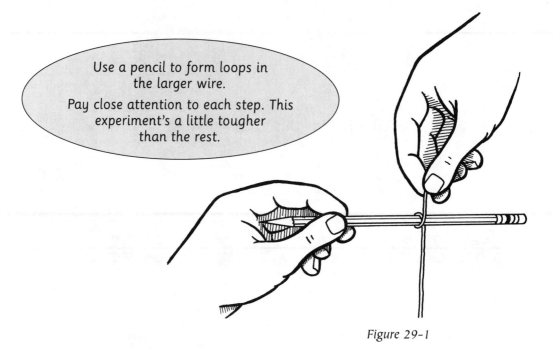

Figure 29-1

5   Extend the free end of the wire out from the block for a lead.

6   Repeat Steps 2 through 5 with the 26-gauge wire. The loops should be turned so that a shaft can be inserted through each opening. (Figure 29-2)

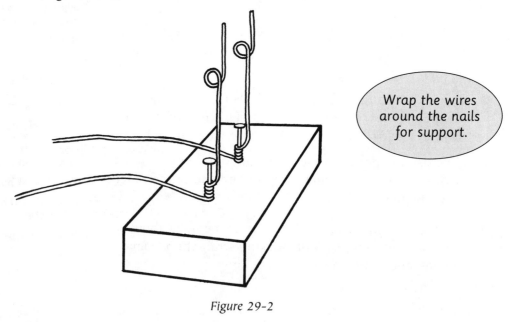

Figure 29-2

7 Wrap the 26-gauge wire around the marker about 10 times to form a coil. Leave about 2 inches (5 cm) of each end free for leads. Now loop one free end tightly around one side of the coil two or three times to keep the wires together. (Figure 29-3)

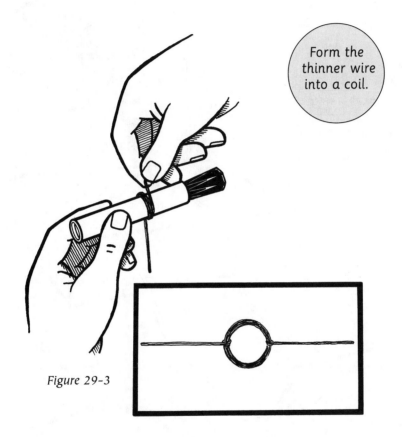

Form the thinner wire into a coil.

Figure 29-3

8 Repeat the step with the other lead, fastening it directly across the coil on the other lead.

9 Sand the varnish from each lead up to the point where it fastens to the coil. Straighten each lead so that it extends straight out from the coil.

10 Insert the batteries into the holder, and connect the leads from the holder to the 22-gauge leads coming from the nails.

117

11 Thread the leads from the coil through the loops fastened to the nails.
    Now hold the magnet near the coil and spin the coil with your
    fingertip. What happens? (Figure 29-4)

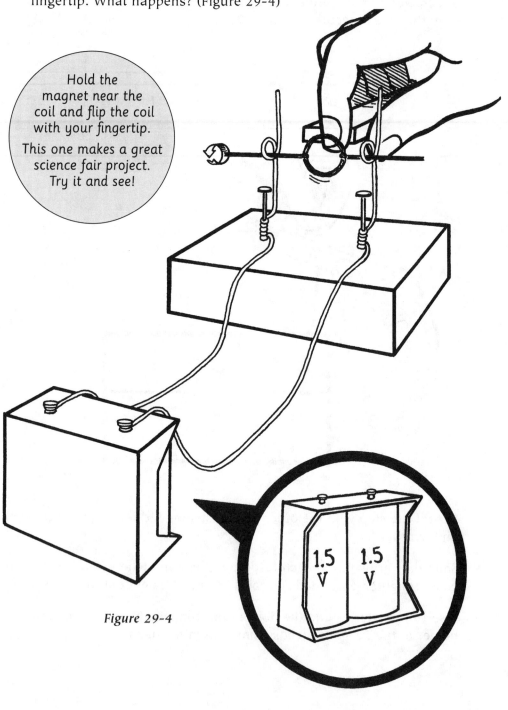

Hold the magnet near the coil and flip the coil with your fingertip.

This one makes a great science fair project. Try it and see!

1.5 V   1.5 V

Figure 29-4

118

> *Now if you could just find a car in which to put our motor, you could get out of here!*

WHAT HAPPENED?

Current from the batteries travels through the 22-gauge wire to the copper coil and creates a magnetic field. The magnetic field from the magnet opposes the field of the coil and causes the coil to turn. If the current continues to flow without interruption or changing direction, the coil will align itself with the opposing field and stay in that position.

In a manufactured motor, the current changes direction each half-turn of the coil. This change of direction keeps pushing the coil along, and the motor turns. In your motor, the current flows only in one direction. But the leads from the coil bounce as the coil spins, and the connection where the leads touch the small loops breaks, interrupting the current. The momentum of the coil keeps it spinning until the leads touch the loops and the current flows again.

The motor you made was only for demonstration, but small motors that can be put to use are available from electronic stores. What could you build with one of these motors? How many motors would a robot use?

GUESS WHAT?

★ Electric motors can convert about 90 percent of the electrical energy into mechanical energy.

★ Electric motors come in all sizes, from fractional horsepower to almost 100,000 horsepower.

119

GLOSSARY

absolute zero The lower limit on physically obtainable temperatures. Equal to −459.67°F or −273.15°C.

alternating current Current that regularly reverses its direction, flowing first in one direction, then in the other. Abbreviated *AC*.

ampere A unit used in measuring electrical current. Usually called an "amp."

aurora borealis (uh-ROAR-uh boor-ree-AL-liss.) Also called the Northern Lights. A phenomenon that can be seen in certain northern regions, such as Scotland and Alaska. The aurora borealis appears as dancing streaks of various illuminated hues across the sky. It is caused by a buildup of electrons and protons that collide with gas molecules, which become excited and give off radiation. Something similar that can be seen near the south pole is called the *aurora australis*.

circuit breaker A safety switch installed in a circuit that automatically interrupts the flow of electricity if the current exceeds a certain amount. Once tripped, a circuit breaker can be manually reset.

compass An instrument that uses a magnetic needle, swinging freely, to show directions.

conductor A material, usually copper wire, used to carry an electrical current.

direct current An electrical current that flows in only one direction. Abbreviated *DC*.

electrical circuit An electrical conductor forming a continuous path, allowing current to flow from a power source through some device using electricity and back to the source.

electromagnet A coil wound on a soft iron core. When a current runs through the coil, the coil becomes magnetized.

electron A tiny particle that carries a negative charge. Electrons, along with neutrons and protons, make up atoms.

electroscope An instrument used to detect a small electrical charge. It consists of two strips of metal foil suspended in a glass container. When charged, the foil strips repel each other.

electrostatic charge A charge of static electricity.

filaments The wires inside a lightbulb that conduct energy.

fluorescent The property of a phosphor that will produce light while it is being radiated with energy such as ultraviolet rays.

fuse A safety device installed in a circuit designed to interrupt the flow of electricity should the current exceed a predetermined amount. A fuse cannot be reused.

galvanometer A meter that detects very small amounts of electrical current and voltage. It is made up of a magnetic needle or a coil in a magnetic field.

generator A rotating device that provides a source of electrical energy. A generator converts mechanical energy into electrical energy. Compare with *motor*.

ground wire A wire that provides an easier path for the electrical current. The wire goes into the earth, causing the electricity to be safely conducted to the ground, away from the circuit. Ground wires are important because they prevent shock hazards.

gyrocompass A compass containing at least one gyroscope that is used by large ships to navigate. A gyrocompass is more accurate than a magnetic compass because it is unaffected by magnetism and points *true north*.

horsepower A unit for measuring the power of motors. The term originally comes from the amount that horses could haul at a given rate.

incandescent Glowing with intense heat. An *incandescent lamp* uses a filament to give off light. The filament is heated by an electrical current.

induction The process by which an electrical or magnetic effect is produced in a conductor or magnetic body when it is exposed to the magnetic field of an electrical current.

insulation A nonconducting material used to cover wires and components to remove shock hazards and to prevent short circuits.

insulator A nonconductor, usually made of glass or porcelain, for insulating and supporting electric wires.

magnet Any piece of certain kinds of material, such as iron, that has the property of attracting like materials.

magnetic field A physical, and invisible, force field produced by a moving electrical charge.

magnetic north The direction a magnetic compass will point when the compass's needle is pointing to the "N" on its dial. The magnetic north pole is not the "real" north pole, but instead, is 1,000 miles (1,600 km) from it. Compare with *true north*.

magnetic storm A sizable disturbance of the earth's magnetic field thought to be caused by the solar wind and solar flares.

millivolt One thousandth of a volt.

motor A machine for converting electric energy into mechanical energy. Compare with *generator*.

neutral The condition of a charged object when the positive and negative charges are equal.

ohm The unit used to measure resistance in a circuit.

parallel circuit A circuit that contains two paths for electrical current supplied by one voltage source.

phosphor A fluorescent substance that gives off light after exposure to radiant energy. Also, it is the substance used to coat the inside of a fluorescent lamp.

polarity Attraction toward an object, often in a specific direction.

poles Electrodes, or terminals on a battery; one end of a magnet.

potentiometer A device used to control or regulate electrical current.

proton A tiny particle that carries a positive charge. Protons, along with neutrons and electrons, make up atoms.

quark A subatomic particle (meaning smaller than an atom) that is even smaller than both protons and electrons.

resistance The property of an electrical circuit that opposes the flow of current through the circuit.

rheostat A variable resistor used to control electrical current.

semiconductor A solid whose ability to conduct electricity is less than a conductor's but greater than an insulator's.

series circuit A circuit that has only one path for the current.

short circuit A connection that occurs when the electricity accidentally takes a path other than the desired path.

solenoid (Pronounced SO-la-noyd.) A coil of wire that carries a current and acts like a magnet. Solenoids are often used as switches to control mechanical devices such as valves.

static electricity Electricity at rest, or a buildup of an electrical charge.

superconductor A conductor cooled to very low temperatures that loses its resistance to an electrical current. It can conduct electricity with zero resistance.

thermocouple A pair of dissimilar metals welded together at one end. When the welded end is heated, a small DC voltage develops across the open ends. This voltage is used to signal controlling devices.

124

true north   The actual north of the earth, unaffected by the earth's magnetic field. Compare with *magnetic north*.

voltage   The electrical pressure, measured in volts, at which a circuit operates.

INDEX

130

ABOUT THE GUY WHO WROTE THIS BOOK

A keen observer of nature and an avid follower of scientific advances, author Robert W. Wood injects his own special brand of fun into children's physics. His *Physics for Kids* series has been through 13 printings, and he has written more than a dozen other science books. His innovative work has been featured in major newspapers and magazines.